Creating Career Programs in a Liberal Arts Context

Mary Ann F. Rehnke, *Editor*
Council of Independent Colleges

NEW DIRECTIONS FOR HIGHER EDUCATION
MARTIN KRAMER, *Editor-in-Chief*
University of California, Berkeley

Number 57, Spring 1987

Paperback sourcebooks in
The Jossey-Bass Higher Education Series

Jossey-Bass Inc., Publishers
San Francisco • London

Mary Ann F. Rehnke (ed.).
Creating Career Programs in a Liberal Arts Context.
New Directions for Higher Education, no. 57.
Volume XV, number 1.
San Francisco: Jossey-Bass, 1987.

New Directions for Higher Education
Martin Kramer, *Editor-in-Chief*

New Directions for Higher Education is published quarterly
by Jossey-Bass Inc., Publishers (publication number USPS
990-880). *New Directions* is numbered sequentially—please
order extra copies by sequential number. The volume and issue
numbers above are included for the convenience of libraries.
Second-class postage paid at San Francisco, California, and at
additional mailing offices. POSTMASTER: Send address changes to
Jossey-Bass Inc., Publishers, 433 California Street, San Francisco,
California 94104.

Editorial correspondence should be sent to the Editor-in-Chief,
Martin Kramer, 2807 Shasta Road, Berkeley, California 94708.

Library of Congress Catalog Card Number LC 85-644752

International Standard Serial Number ISSN 0271-0560

International Standard Book Number ISBN 1-55542-962-9

Cover art by WILLI BAUM

Manufactured in the United States of America

Ordering Information

The paperback sourcebooks listed below are published quarterly and can be ordered either by subscription or single copy.

Subscriptions cost $48.00 per year for institutions, agencies, and libraries. Individuals can subscribe at the special rate of $36.00 per year *if payment is by personal check.* (Note that the full rate of $48.00 applies if payment is by institutional check, even if the subscription is designated for an individual.) Standing orders are accepted.

Single copies are available at $11.95 when payment accompanies order. (California, New Jersey, New York, and Washington, D.C., residents please include appropriate sales tax.) For billed orders, cost per copy is $11.95 plus postage and handling.

Substantial discounts are offered to organizations and individuals wishing to purchase bulk quantities of Jossey-Bass sourcebooks. Please inquire.

Please note that these prices are for the academic year 1986–1987 and are subject to change without notice. Also, some titles may be out of print and therefore not available for sale.

To ensure correct and prompt delivery, all orders must give either the *name of an individual* or an *official purchase order number.* Please submit your order as follows:

Subscriptions: specify series and year subscription is to begin.
Single Copies: specify sourcebook code (such as, HE1) and first two words of title.

Mail orders for United States and Possessions, Australia, New Zealand, Canada, Latin America, and Japan to:
Jossey-Bass Inc., Publishers
433 California Street
San Francisco, California 94104

Mail orders for all other parts of the world to:
Jossey-Bass Limited
28 Banner Street
London EC1Y 8QE

New Directions for Higher Education Series
Martin Kramer, *Editor-in-Chief*

HE1 *Facilitating Faculty Development,* Mervin Freedman
HE2 *Strategies for Budgeting,* George Kaludis
HE3 *Services for Students,* Joseph Katz

Contents

Editor's Notes

Should our campus add an undergraduate career program to the curriculum? Will the program be appropriate for our institution? Although job opportunities are currently plentiful for these graduates, will this still be true in six years when our first graduates enter the job market? What is the best career preparation for students, given statistical data indicating that most students have at least four careers during their lives? How will the tenured liberal arts faculty react to the new program and new faculty? What legal issues will be involved? Does the program need to be accredited? How do we ensure that a high-quality program is developed that will meet the needs and standards of the profession? Since an increasing portion of the college-age population is composed of women and minorities, how does the campus ensure that they will be attracted to and retained in career programs that frequently have been the province of white males? What is the planning process for developing the new program? Each chapter in this sourcebook focuses on an answer to one of these questions.

Answering these questions appropriately is significant for higher education institutions for two reasons. First, 50 percent of our undergraduates, according to data from the Carnegie Foundation for the Advancement of Teaching (1985), major in occupational or professional fields. These students are increasingly preoccupied with preparation for jobs. In institutions especially sensitive to market demand, the Liberal Arts Colleges II, almost three-fourths of undergraduates major in occupational fields.

Second, the institution choosing to add a new career program is committing itself to a major investment that will affect financial resources, faculty morale, institutional mission, and community relations. The college must have thoroughly explored the positive and negative aspects of adding a new program. This book may assist campuses in avoiding inappropriate additions to the curriculum as well as in strengthening educational programs.

This sourcebook may be used in three ways. First, campuses may wish to explore how they may best prepare students to be useful contributors to society. Faculty groups can read the chapters by Marc S. Tucker, Arthur E. Levine, and John Harris, who deal in broad conceptual terms with the topic of careers. These chapters stimulate a discussion of ways other than the provision of a strong major in a specific occupational area in which colleges can prepare students for the world of work. A second way campuses can use this book is in helping to determine whether or not they should add a specific career program. Is a new major in nursing appropriate for the campus? If so, how does the campus go about plan-

1

ning a strong program? Third, this book may be used as a reference tool. A campus administrator can consult the figures in Chapter Six to find the appropriate accrediting body for a new major or can look at how a legal question may be solved by referring to Chapter Five.

To assist readers in thinking through the possible adoption of a career program, the format of this book moves from the general to the specific—from conceptual issues, to topics that should be addressed early in the planning process, and then to those program refinements that would be covered when the campus has definitely decided to develop the career program.

The volume begins in Chapter One with an overview of education and the economy by Marc S. Tucker. Given two views of the evolving economy, Tucker believes that the one that will dominate will require colleges to revitalize their liberal arts curricula and create programs of performanced-based models rather than preparing students for highly specialized careers.

In Chapter Two Arthur E. Levine describes the accidental revolution on campuses created when colleges introduce career programs and the divisive debates that occur over the definition of an educated person. He places career programs in a historical context, illustrating the traditionally dual role of education in providing students with the tools for intellectual advancement and for serving a useful role in society. He traces changes in the curriculum and the definition of an educated person, calling on educators to stretch the traditional definition of an educated person to meet new marketplace demands.

In Chapter Three Allen P. Splete covers the presidential perspective on career programs and raises issues the chief executive officer must address when the possibility of adding a career program is first considered. Questions of need, mission compatibility, and economics arise. Splete discusses philosophical as well as practical considerations that the president must consider before embarking on a full-fledged planning process for a new program.

If the program appears to be a good possibility for the campus, Philip C. Winstead explains in Chapter Four how to proceed with the planning process. Having appointed someone to be in charge of the planning process, the campus would follow a planning model that covers needs assessment, future considerations, institutional mission, specific program planning, resource allocations, and how to gain support from key people. Within this overall planning model, a feasibility study would be conducted. Winstead also indicates sources of data for use in planning.

In the planning process institutions will need to address specific concerns, such as legal issues or assessment considerations. Chapters Five to Ten address topics that arise in the planning process.

Legal concerns regarding faculty contracts, student rights, licensure and accreditation, both in and out of state, as well as policy recommendations are covered in Chapter Five by David J. Figuli, R. Claire Guthrie, and Andrew L. Abrams.

To determine the accreditation, licensure, or certification requirements of a specific professional program, consult the charts developed by Marjorie Peace Lenn in Chapter Six. They indicate which accrediting body to contact for further information about the career area, the accrediting scope of that organization, and whether certification or licensure is tied to graduation from an accredited program.

Because assessment is a growing concern of accrediting bodies, colleges and universities, state governments, and federal agencies, John Harris in Chapter Seven stresses the need to build assessment into programs at the onset. He illustrates how to create an instructional system to certify that graduates are competent and provide feedback regarding the program's curriculum, instructional methods, faculty, and admission procedures. He also explains how to use assessment for student guidance.

In Chapter Eight, Carol J. Carter explains strategies for retaining women and minority students in career programs.

In all aspects of creating a new program, the faculty play a key role; their developmental needs are the focus of Chapter Nine by Roger G. Baldwin. He argues that the effectiveness of the institution will be enhanced by appropriate assistance for faculty in adjusting to the new program. The program may give faculty an opportunity to expand their teaching and advising strategies, write grants, or move beyond their discipline as they develop skills supportive of the new program. He discusses the appropriate use of adjunct and temporary faculty as well as the needs of displaced faculty.

Faculty, too, are the focus of Chapter Ten by Joan S. Stark. She argues for early consideration by the campus community of the unique characteristics of professional programs as a first step in creating a harmonious relationship with liberal arts faculty. Career programs, she points out, differ from liberal arts disciplines in their relationships with the external environment and in the background of their faculty. However, there is an opportunity for integration and compatibility between the two program areas when considering educational outcomes, curricular debates, and educational activities.

Whether campuses use this volume in planning a career program, determining that a program is inappropriate for their institution, or exploring what it means to provide a useful education for a student today, this sourcebook is intended to strengthen the curricula of our colleges and universities in order to provide students with a liberal as well as useful education.

Mary Ann F. Rehnke
Editor

4

Reference

Carnegie Foundation for the Advancement of Teaching. "Change Trendlines: Tracking the Undergraduate Major." *Change*, March/April 1985, pp. 30-33.

Mary Ann F. Rehnke is director of annual programs at the Council of Independent Colleges. She has served in administrative positions at the American Association for Higher Education, the College of St. Catherine, Daemen College, and Northern Kentucky University, where she was also a faculty member.

The changing economy may in time produce fundamental changes in the market for higher education.

The College Market

Marc S. Tucker

This chapter explores how to think about the way the market for higher education may develop over the years ahead in light of the evolving structure of the national economy and how it reflects the changing demography of our society.

It is an essay in the first person because there is nothing particularly scientific or even scholarly about this exploration. We currently do not know enough about the complex forces at work to make accurate predictions of the form of or demand for particular college programs and curriculum offerings ten to fifteen years hence. In fact, such matters are inherently unknowable and are rather the subject for modest speculation.

The Demand for Educated Labor

The driving force in determining the demand for college education is probably the economy's demand for educated labor. People offset the expected cost of a college education—in direct expenses and foregone earnings—against the gains they expect in lifetime earnings. Although population groups differ in their belief that education pays off or that they personally can reap the benefits (witness the large percentage of Asian Americans and low percentage of blacks attending college, for example), the human capital literature tells us that, on the whole, people are surprisingly accurate the world over in their estimates of the economic benefits of education, and they act on these assessments.

M.A.F. Rehnke (ed.). *Creating Career Programs in a Liberal Arts Context.*
New Directions for Higher Education, no. 57. San Francisco: Jossey-Bass, Spring 1987.

So, what do we know about the likely returns to personal investments in higher education in the years ahead? To answer this question, we need to understand the evolving structure of the American economy—no small undertaking, and one that is the subject of enormous controversy.

There are those who believe that advancing technology will inevitably result in the progressive "deskilling" of work for most people—that is, that manual tasks will require less skill or be taken over entirely by machines and that increasingly sophisticated information technology will, among other things, eliminate the need for most middle managers. In this vision of the future, there will be only a few highly skilled and well-paid people at the top of our society, and the middle level will virtually disappear. Anyone subscribing to this view must surely believe that the number of our colleges would be greatly reduced over the next two decades or so.

Fortunately, there is as yet no evidence to support this gloomy view of the future. The Bureau of Labor Statistics (BLS) data show that the proportion of professional and technical jobs in the work force is increasing and that the proportion of clerical and other low-skill job classifications is decreasing (Rosenthal, 1985). The BLS predicts that this trend will continue. The pessimists could turn out to be right, however, if public policy takes a bad turn.

Perhaps the best way to think about the likely role of education in the future of our economy is to look backward, to analyze the sources of strength in the American economy over the years and to focus on the challenges to that strength.

Competition and Skills in the Smokestack Age

The vast expansion of compulsory education in the early part of this century made it possible to provide the basic skills of reading, writing, arithmetic, and citizenship to large numbers of poorly educated people who came to the city from farms or from Europe. Many of these people entered factories in which enormous sums were invested in advanced machinery designed to make the best use of a relatively low-skill work force. The work was routine and so were the skills required to do the work. In the early years much of the technology was borrowed from Europe. Later on our education system was expanded to provide for an elite of scientists, engineers, and managers who could make the system work from the top, but the vast majority of the work force continued to need and have only basic skills. Domestic markets were expanding so fast that the cost of big investments in plants and equipment could be spread over very large quantities of finished products.

In the system I have just described, capital investment was synonymous with investment in plants and equipment. The idea was to reduce the cost of labor in relation to total cost in order to improve productivity and keep prices down. Although this system worked with success for decades, it is now under attack. The longer we cling to it, the more grim the economic outlook will be, for the following reasons.

The cost of telecommunications and transportation are now so low that finished goods and services can be sold in markets all over the world, independent of where they originate. The most advanced production technologies and the capital necessary to purchase them are now available to countries we have long regarded as backward. Many of those countries now meet or exceed our capacity to provide the basic skills to their work force. Those work forces often regard wage levels one-tenth of our own as high. Furthermore, they are willing to work as much as twice as many hours for those wages as are our workers.

The implication is clear. Firms in this country that continue to base their operations on the use of domestic low-skill, low-pay labor cannot compete. They are, and will continue to be, forced to automate those jobs fully or export them to foreign countries in which they build their own facilities or from whom they purchase products or services to be sold in this country. All of this is actually happening at frightening speed.

Although individual firms can succeed by moving operations overseas or by becoming marketing agents for foreign firms, the country cannot. The enormous trade deficit cannot continue indefinitely. Eventually, what we buy from others must be matched by what we sell to others. If we cannot sell more, we will have to buy less, and our standard of living will fall until it matches that of our less well-to-do competitors.

Competition and Skills in an Integrated World Economy

If others are willing to do what we do and to charge much less for it, we can only justify higher relative wages by doing something they cannot do, something that will justify the higher price we charge for our labor.

In a nutshell, the answer is a high-skill, high-wage economy. Only by creating an economy based on very highly educated workers who are backed up by the most sophisticated technology available will we be able to create products and services of such great value that they will command a premium price on world markets.

In a world in which capital and technology move across international borders quickly and easily, only the skills of workers and the capacity of management to put those skills to good use will account for competitive advantage, for differences in national income. This is because it takes decades to make and reap the rewards of investments in the capacities of people, and once those investments are made, the people in whom they reside tend to stay within national borders much more so than money and technology. This view entails a sea of change in economic philosophy, business practice, and national cultural values.

Changes in investment philosophy are essential. Both manufacturing and service industries will require far higher levels of investment than they do now. To succeed, both law offices and glass factories will have to employ very well-educated people who are supported by very sophisticated machinery that makes it possible for them to operate at peak efficiency. These people include not just senior managers and professionals but people in other classifications as well. Plant foremen will turn from tasks that can be learned quickly through observation to tasks that require an understanding of complex industrial processes that cannot be seen and therefore cannot be learned by observing others. Clerical staff in service industries will find routine tasks being taken over by machines and will be employable only if they, too, understand the firm's business and operations, exercise independent judgment, and solve unusual problems. Conceptual thinking will become a basic requirement, as will real understanding of abstract subjects. Very little that people do will be routine, if they are to continue to justify high wages on a worldwide pay scale.

It costs a lot of money to create a well-educated person. It also costs a lot of money to back up all those well-educated people with the equipment they will need to work efficiently. The result is that a successful economy will be extremely investment intensive. Business and government policies will have to be based, not on the view that capital investment means reducing investment in people but rather on the view that capital investment means investing much greater sums in both people and equipment.

Investing in Oneself

But will people invest in themselves? Until now the incentives to do so have been relatively weak. High school dropouts from Detroit who joined the United Auto Workers and went to work in the auto industry could confidently expect to make more in a few years than the Ivy League graduate who went on to become an assistant professor of sociology at Yale. But this is much less likely to be true in the future if our economy is successful. In the future pay will increasingly be a function of what people know, of their education and ability to put their education to work.

This circumstance implies an extraordinary change in American cultural values. Although we certainly have intellectual elites, the culture as a whole does not place the same value on education and learning as do some of our most determined competitors, not least of which are those on the Pacific rim. Our national capacity to make the changes we must make to remain competitive may be more severely tested by this lack of regard for learning than by any other factor. Still, Americans have undergone some truly astonishing revolutions in values in the past, and their ability to change ought not to be underestimated.

It should be clear by now why I believe that our economic future is inherently unknowable. It is not difficult to determine the form of the economy needed if we are to remain competitive. What is impossible to know is whether Americans will make the necessary wrenching changes in economic policy, business practice, education policy, and cultural values. But there is cause for optimism, I believe, mostly because our political system has a record of forcing necessary adjustments in public policy just when the hour is darkest; we tend to rise to the occasion.

Demography and the Demand for College

But where is this very well-educated work force to come from? The basic demographic realities are now known to every discerning newspaper reader. People of college-going age are declining absolutely and as a proportion of the population as a whole. In fact, people of working age are declining as a proportion of the population as a whole. The number of children in school is rising faster than the rate of general population increase, but almost all of the increase in elementary and secondary students is coming from poor and minority families—those that have until now proven the most difficult to educate.

What can we say, then, about the prospects facing our colleges? If the country as a whole, through whatever mechanism, develops the will to face up to its economic problems, then it is highly likely that the demand for a college education will increase substantially, because it will be progressively clearer that economic prospects depend on educational attainment.

Demand is likely to come not just from those who are graduating from high school but also from those already in the work force who want to improve their prospects. The extent of this demand is likely, at least in part, to be a function of public policy (the extent to which taxpayers choose to subsidize the reeducation of the work force) and of private policy (the extent to which employers believe that it is in their interest to subsidize the reeducation and continuing education of their workers).

Not only is it likely that people older than the typical college student will continue to swell the ranks of college-goers, it is also likely that people below the age of eighteen will be increasingly interested in going to college. It is already the case that some colleges, not content with limiting themselves to the traditional market, are positioning themselves to expand market share by recruiting students to begin college before they have completed high school. Some states are now making it possible for high school students to attend college and get credit for high school at the same time. The students are less bored and progress faster; the state saves money.

So it may make sense for former automobile assembly workers and tenth graders to go to college. But what about the Black or Chicano drop-out who lives in Los Angeles? As the costs of dependency rise and the need to devote an increasing share of our resources to nonproductive investment increases, the demand to educate the uneducated will increase, too, as a matter of enlightened self-interest.

So the students will be there, but they will be far more heterogeneous than they are now, much more resistant to the established organization and culture of our colleges than today's students. And they will be more demanding. Most college students now and in the past have tended to take college as it comes, meaning that college faculty and administration have enormous latitude in determining what the college experience means. This situation is likely to change.

Clients of Higher Education

As college costs continue to rise faster than inflation, the burden of college loans rises. As the debt burden increases, there is mounting pressure for the state to take over an increasing share of the costs. There is also increasing motivation for students to leave full-time study early and combine continued study with employment, often at the employer's expense. As the cost of college borne by the state and by employers rises, they will increasingly demand that the education they are buying meets their standards and that it be efficiently provided. What has happened in health care, in other words, is likely to happen in higher education. It is already happening, as attested to by the recent interest of state authorities in developing methods to assess the accomplishments of college graduates from state-funded institutions. They want to know if the state is getting its money's worth. As private firms bear an increasing share of the cost of education, contracts between higher education institutions and firms to provide education to employees are becoming more common. It is quite likely that large firms will be increasingly interested in contracting for the services of higher education institutions in coming years. New sources of students will therefore come at the price of institutional autonomy for many colleges and will require great changes in curriculum and organization for virtually all.

What sort of changes in curriculum will occur? Is it not likely that these economic changes and the increasing role of institutional clients will drive the curriculum toward ever more vocational objectives, that these trends herald the demise of the liberal arts curriculum? I think not.

On the contrary, I think there is every reason to believe that the forces described will lead to the rebirth of the liberal arts curriculum. First of all, history is on the side of the liberal arts. Over the years, vocationalism has predominated when college graduates have been in oversupply, as in recent years, and the liberal arts have won out when demand outran supply, as predicted for the years ahead.

But more to the point, the character of the work ahead will favor people of the sort described by most after-dinner speakers these days: people who are flexible, learn fast, and are capable of independent problem solving.

Before the arts and sciences faculty relaxes, however, I should point out that I believe all too few arts and sciences courses are taught in a way calculated to develop these capacities. Course titles do not add up to a well-educated person. I employ new graduates from well-known colleges and so do many of my acquaintances. Almost all of us have a hard time finding new graduates with the qualities described. One can only conclude that the colleges that meet employers' tests in the years ahead will be those that have given a lot of thought not just to the names of the courses they teach but to the qualities they want to see in their graduates. It is only a small leap from that point to the desire of an employer to see how graduates perform on an exit assessment that measures such qualities. When that assessment is produced and administered to the graduates of many colleges, it will have a very large market.

Through a Glass Darkly

As income becomes ever more closely connected with education and the costs of education continue to outpace inflation, it is inevitable that higher education policymakers and their institutional clients will ask progressively sharper questions about what they are getting for their money. Degree-based systems for certifying competence are likely to give way to performance-based systems and performance-based systems will be used to allocate resources in the interest of increasing the efficiency with which an increasingly valuable resource, the faculties of higher education, are being used.

It follows from this analysis that college officials who define the planning and marketing task in terms of divining the professional career opportunities people will want to prepare for are barking up the wrong tree. They will be chasing the will-o'-the-wisp of cyclical supply and demand, and the cycles will get progressively shorter. What this means in plain terms is that just as a college and its competitors expands its business curriculum, demand for people with baccalaureates in business will decline and there will be a growing oversupply. Far better to offer an unspecialized product of very high quality at a competitive price to well-known clients.

But this is all seen through a glass darkly. The context is so complex that the future is inherently unknowable. My advice is probably worth no more than that of many people with whom I disagree deeply. What may be most important therefore is the preservation of great variety in higher education. Only in this way can we be sure that mutations take place fast enough and range far enough to guarantee that some set of institutions will be producing the education that is needed at any point in time. Natural selection is a stern master, but we know that it works.

Reference

Rosenthal, N. H. "The Shrinking Middle Class." *The Monthly Labor Review,* 1985, *108* (3), 3-10.

Marc S. Tucker is executive director of the Carnegie Forum on Education and the Economy. He has written widely on education policy issues.

*Career education has been a consistent and persistent purpose
of American higher education, but that purpose has to be
continually updated to respond to changes in the larger society.*

Career Education: A Prospective, a Retrospective, and a Few Guesses

Arthur E. Levine

In 1973, California State College at San Bernadino experienced a 55 percent decline in applications. Adminstrators and faculty were flabbergasted. After a rash of meetings and proposals the college voted to scrap many of the old liberal arts notions. It dropped comprehensive examinations, a readings program, and various requirements in general education, foreign language, and writing. The college embraced a more vocational mission (Cheit, 1975). The business curriculum was expanded. New programs were adopted in criminal justice, nursing, and health science. Graduate instruction was offered in policy studies, management, and teaching. Enrollments promptly jumped.

The San Bernadino experience is being repeated on campuses all across the country today. The simple fact is that the American college is moving, due to market pressure, toward increasingly vocational missions. Enrollments in career-oriented fields—business, health, engineering—are booming. In contrast, the liberal arts, historically the centerpiece of American collegiate education, is experiencing dramatic reverses.

All across the nation professional and technical majors have come to dominate the baccalaureate. A majority of colleges have adopted or

M.A.F. Rehnke (ed.). *Creating Career Programs in a Liberal Arts Context.*
New Directions for Higher Education, no. 57. San Francisco: Jossey-Bass, Spring 1987.

expanded their program in health science and business. Engineering and education are growing quickly, too.

At the same time, undergraduate education is becoming more specialized. Students are taking many more classes in their majors. Academic departments—from English to engineering—are requiring more major courses for the bachelor of science degree. A rising number of schools are offering double major options, which permit students to do little more than concentrate on required courses rather than receive a broad education during four years of college.

Also, a variety of mechanisms are being introduced to provide academic credit for courses taken at postsecondary vocational and technical schools. Some institutions accept as the equivalent of collegiate study programs in air conditioning and television repair. A majority of colleges also grant credit for work experience in amounts varying from a few credits to most or all of a degree.

In aggregate these changes amount to nothing less than an academic revolution. The irony is that it has been an accidental revolution—one that has occurred in a haphazard fashion, more by indecision than design. Few colleges have made such a deliberate choice as did San Bernadino. Most are still attempting to resolve the issues.

Divisive Debate

A heated debate is raging on campuses from coast to coast. Faced with a troubled job market and demands for more practical instruction, the academic community is deeply divided over the place of and even the appropriateness of vocational education for institutions of higher learning. More than 60 percent of faculty say career preparation is not an important outcome of college. In contrast, nearly 70 percent of undergraduates consider it essential.

The issue of vocationalism is mired today in a miasma of diversionary concerns. On one level vocationalism has become not a debate about education but a battle over turf and resources. It is a casualty in a fight between underenrolled liberal arts departments and understaffed professional and vocational fields for enrollments and faculty lines. It is a fatality in an age of retrenchment when existing departments are vetoing the creation of new programs in the hope of preserving their limited resources.

At another level vocationalism has become a referendum on tradition. New career-oriented programs are being perfunctorily rejected at some schools, not because they are educationally inappropriate, although this is certainly possible, but because they are different. We are reminded of the Oxbridge debate on whether history was a fit discipline for study. In the end history was rejected as too inconsequential a subject.

At a third level vocationalism has come to be a code word meaning the propping up of sagging colleges. Too often institutions consider and adopt new career programs, not because they are educationally merited but because they may attract more students. By contrast well-heeled schools too often express disdain for vocational programs.

Historic Debate

This debate is by no means new. There is a long-cherished myth that threads itself through the history of higher education. It holds that colleges and universities were originally rooted wholly in the great intellectual traditions of their age but more recently have turned away from this mission to the more practical and vocational concerns of the day.

Robert Hutchins thought this "change" occurred at the turn of this century with the rise of "schools of journalism, business, librarianship, social service, education, dentistry, nursing, forestry, diplomacy, pharmacy, veterinary surgery, and public administration" (Hutchins, 1936, pp. 33-34). Thorstein Veblen attributed it to an earlier event: the adoption of the free elective system after the Civil War. Cardinal Newman blamed the enlightenment, citing both the French university and the activities of John Locke and his disciples. And before him in first century B.C. Dionysius of Halicarnassus felt the Greeks were responsible for encouraging students to prematurely specialize.

The point is, if educational history teaches us anything, it is that schooling is a practical matter. Educational institutions, from kindergartens to colleges, are intended to teach students about the existing world of which they are a part and to give them the intellectual skills to perform in that world in a productive and socially beneficial manner.

Viewed from this perspective higher learning has always been considered useful. Our first formal universities nearly a millennium ago were, as Samuel Eliot Morrison put it, "distinctly purposeful" (Morrison, 1935, p. 7). The University of Salerno, the first institution of record, was a medical school. The universities that followed in its wake—Bologna, Paris, Oxford, Cambridge and the rest—offered only four courses of study: law, medicine, theology, and the arts. The arts curriculum (the undergradute or foundation program), teaching the classical trivium and to a lesser extent quadrivium, was also practical. In the words of historian Nathan Schachner (1962, pp. 124-125), such instruction "was not to be considered as a medium of culture; it was something utilitarian. It was a means of learning the universal Latin and the rules of Logic, so that the student could enter the professional schools." The training was, in fact, vocational, and jobs lay at the end.

The American college, a descendant of this medieval university emphasizing undergraduate education, followed in the same tradition.

Eighteenth-century historians Samuel Davis and Gilbert Tennent concluded that the most urgent reason for founding the prerevolutionary colleges was to train a learned clergy (Davis and Tennent, 1976). This was an explicit rationale prominently featured in the promotional and legal documentation of these earliest institutions, such as Harvard, the College of William and Mary, and Yale. Since that time the program of the American college has undergone many and varied permutations, but the commitment to useful education has remained a persistent and consistent theme. It would be a mistake, however, to conclude that higher education is nothing more than a pale reflection of the job market.

Compatibility of Education and Vocation

For most of higher education's history there has been a splendid compatibility between the collegiate vision of an educated person and the vocations of college graduates. Higher education graduates have generally attained positions of privilege and power.

From the first the accepted mission of the college was not to train monkish churchmen but to educate community leaders, members of the prestige professions of which the clergy was foremost. There was wide agreement that the practical education required for all professions was a classical education.

The curriculum of the day, a mirror of the college's practical purposes, consisted of just twelve subjects: logic, Greek, Hebrew, rhetoric, divinity catechetical, history, nature of plants, ethics and politics, Aramaic, arithmetic, astronomy, Syriac. It was a comprehensive treatment of the knowledge of the era and provided students with an education in both breadth and depth. It taught a common language and a common Christian perspective. It prepared students for the world in which they would live and work. Simply stated, the goal of the early American college was to provide a broad education for a narrow range of jobs.

Here's the point. Students of the early colleges, just as the student generation before them, were preparing for productive work. But the education they received was determined not by the marketplace but by the college's vision of an educated person.

Societal Changes Affect Education

As the nation grew and the democratic tradition blossomed, this comfortable compatibility between education and vocation shifted. The number of students going to college grew, and a more economically and socially diverse group filled the classrooms. America's colleges, numbering nine on the eve of the Revolution, had increased by more than fourteenfold at the time of the Civil War.

Most significant, perhaps, was the change in the workplace. Outward expansion and an industrial revolution opened up dramatic new possibilities for young Americans. The changing contours of the nation that challenged the tradition of higher education were vividly described by Robert Heilbroner (1977, p. 49).

By every standard, the country was vastly richer in 1860 than it had been in 1800. Population had increased from 5 million to 31 million. In 1800 there was no city over 70,000; now there were already two cities with more than 500,000 people. In Washington's time 95 percent of the population lived in rural settings; in Lincoln's time the figure had fallen to 80 percent—one-fifth of the nation was already "urban." And whereas only 350,000 persons worked in factories or mills or hand trades in 1820 (the earliest date for which we have statistics), by the time of the Civil War there were 2 million men and women laboring in tasks that were neither agricultural nor "service" but industrial.

The college program, which seemed so well suited to the colonies, no longer served a nation in the throes of change. America had been transformed from a theocratic community to a burgeoning industrial society.

A New Curriculum Emerges

In response to changes in the economy and the nation, a new curriculum was shaped to meet new realities. Modern subjects were added. In the eighteenth century instruction was added in mathematics, medicine, and law. Engineering, science, education, and business were products of the next century. Modern languages and laboratory study increasingly became curricular staples. Federal legislation—a Land Grant Act—spurred the development of colleges of agriculture and mechanical arts.

The course of studies became increasingly specialized. As early as 1825 the University of Virginia began to offer undergraduates eight different and distinct courses of study, ranging from ancient languages to medicine and commerce. Specialized nondegree programs called partial courses mushroomed. Institutions such as Harvard and Yale created alternative degrees, a bachelor of science and a bachelor of philosophy, for nonclassical study. In the 1870s Johns Hopkins used two new terms: *majors* and *minors*.

Finally, the dam burst. Through the sheer expansion of subjects and programs, it became impossible for colleges to continue to offer their students a single common curriculum. A free elective movement swept higher education in the last third of the nineteenth century. Colleges abandoned their requirements in favor of student choice.

This dramatic realignment of the curriculum in an attempt to make it more useful was not achieved without a struggle. Yale offered an articulate defense of the classical curriculum that, according to historian Frederick Rudolph (1962), set back reform efforts for a generation. There was a strong conviction that colleges were losing sight of their vision of the educated person. The curriculum was being determined by the marketplace.

This perception was not entirely wrong, but what it overlooked was the recognition that the marketplace had always been an factor in shaping the curriculum of the college. What was different, of course, was the fact that the marketplace was making new demands. Given time, an accommodation between the marketplace and college was reached. The definition of the educated person changed gradually and by degrees. In part this was an adjustment to new social and work conditions, but it was also a response to new academic realities: a quickly and continually expanding universe of knowledge. As well as recognizing the need to train for new vocations, educators saw the limits of a classical core of study seeking to embrace all knowlege and all people. Clearly, there was too much to learn and too many specialized pursuits to prepare for. Some choice was necessary.

The Concept of the New Educated Person

The period from 1865 to about 1910 was a time of drift for the American college. Many different visions of the educated person were tried: the educated person as humanist, the educated person as utilitarian, the educated person as scholar, and so on. By the end of World War I the vision that prevailed was an amalgam that combined the common intellectual and social perspective of the colonial core with the recognized need for specialization. The educated person was hailed as both a generalist and a specialist. The predominant pattern in higher education became general education and a major—and the major quickly came to dominate. Again there was a consistency between the college definition of the educated person and marketplace demands.

Summary

The history of undergraduate education in America has been the story of designing the curriculum to meet the twin goals of intellectual advancement and utility. With the growth of knowledge and changing social conditions, one curriculum grows out of date and another replaces it. Hastings Rashdall (1936, p. 455), the renowned nineteenth-century scholar of the medieval university, put it well when he said "the intelligent artisan educated at a primary school or the half educated man of the world possesses at the present day a great deal more true and useful knowledge than a medieval doctor of divinity." The fact is that the best and most useful education is rendered trivial and impractical by the passage of time. Although the commitment of colleges and universities to practical education has been constant the notion of what is utilitarian—intellectually and socially—is forever in flux. Over the years, educators have argued about how practical a college education should be and debated about what practical education is appropriate to a university. They have battled about the best way to educate, and they have fought about whether curriculums have been designed by the academic community or constructed by workplace demands. But few if any educators have questioned whether a college education should be practical.

Even the well-known dissenters, those who disagreed most strongly with the new vocationalism of their time, such as Day, Newman, Flexner, Hutchins, Barr, and Buchanan, did not oppose practical education. Each claimed instead that concern with specific jobs and technical skills was trivial, even demeaning to a university.

Robert Hutchins (1936) opposed professional schools. He did so not because he felt education should be useless but because the training needed for these new vocations seemed to him inconsistent with the greater usefulness of a classical curriculum. Hutchins wanted a more utilitarian program.

In 1903 W.E.B. DuBois (1969, p. 84) defined the purpose of a college as developing "that fine adjustment between life and the growing knowledge of life, an adjustment which forms the secret of civilization."

In a very real sense the never-ending process of defining what is useful and what is not constitutes humankind's unceasing effort to preserve the critical adjustment between an expanding body of knowledge and a world in which real life is forever changing. For the most part DuBois was correct: It has been a matter of fine adjustment. But periodically it has required something more—a gross refitting. On rare occasions a society changes very greatly and very rapidly so that its institutions, which are by nature slower to act, are left far behind.

The first half of the nineteenth century was such a time. Higher education's vision of the educated person was inconsistent with the society in which its graduates would live; it was left over from a bygone era. A new vision, a reconceptualization of what it meant to be an educated person in a different time under different conditions, was required to keep the college vibrant and productive.

Today America is going through another period of momentous change. The post–Civil War vision of the educated person has became dated and less useful. The American college is at a turning point. The critical question is not which education is most useful but rather how traditions of intellectual inquiry and scholarship can once again be stretched to meet the new marketplace demands. This is the most urgent agenda facing higher education today.

20

References

Cheit, E. F. *The Useful Arts and the Liberal Tradition*. New York: McGraw-Hill, 1975.

Davis, S., and Tennent, G. "Reasons for Founding Colleges in America." In *Annals of America*. Vol. 1. Chicago: Encyclopedia Brittanica, 1976.

DuBois, W.E.B. *The Souls of Black Folk*. New York: New American Library, 1969.

Heilbroner, R. (In collaboration with Aaron Singer). *The Economic Transformation of America*. New York: Harcourt, Brace, Jovanovich, 1977.

Hutchins, R. *Higher Learning in America*. New York: Yale University Press, 1936.

Morrison, S. E. *The Founding of Harvard College*. Cambridge: Harvard University Press, 1935.

Rashdall, H. *The Universities of Europe in the Middle Ages*. Vol. 3. Oxford, England: Oxford University Press, 1936.

Rudolph, F. *American College and University: A History*. New York: Knopf, 1962.

Schachner, N. *The Mediaeval Universities*. New York: A. S. Barnes, 1962.

Arthur E. Levine is president of Bradford College. He is also the author of a number of articles and books on higher education, including Reform of Undergraduate Education *(Jossey-Bass, 1973),* Handbook on Undergraduate Curriculum *(Jossey-Bass, 1978),* When Dreams and Heroes Died *(Jossey-Bass, 1980), and* Opportunity in Adversity *(Jossey-Bass, 1986).*

*When considering new career programs, presidents must
balance need and temptation with economic reality yet have
the courage to take appropriate risks.*

The Presidential Perspective on Mission Review for New Career Programs

Allen P. Splete

College presidents can and do spend sleepless nights over the impact of
adding a career program to an established curriculum, especially when
traditional liberal arts courses and programs have been at the heart of the
college since its founding. The worries of a comprehensive university president parallel those of the small-college president. Colleges of arts and
sciences are also mindful of the job market and of the need to place their
graduates, and these colleges must compete for students with the preprofessional colleges within the same institution. When some nontraditional
courses have been added and the case in question is merely the expansion
or legitimization of a course of study already offered, the issue of adding a
career program may not arise. However, when the proposal is for a new
program that desires legitimate status as an equal partner in the campus
enterprise, it can be cause for a review of the college's mission.

Although the decision to add a career program might seem to be
right for the short term, the long-term consequences are of greater impact,
harder to assess, and much more likely to be detrimental to the stated
mission of the college. A second major concern for presidents is the economic implications, although dollar evaluations may not be possible until

M.A.F. Rehnke (ed.). *Creating Career Programs in a Liberal Arts Context.*
New Directions for Higher Education, no. 57. San Francisco: Jossey-Bass, Spring 1987.

the full debate of noneconomic factors is completed. It is important not to initially jeopardize key discussions on the value of the proposed program and its internal consequences. The outcome may justify the financial risk, or new financing strategies may become obvious in the course of the review process. Conversely, economic realities may prove too great an obstacle, and the program idea may be dropped before any planning is done. Commonly, those colleges that have experienced severe enrollment decline or now confront it will evaluate a career program in light of the proposed benefits for recruitment of students or the promise of new fund-raising resources rather than from the point of view of its effect on the college's mission.

Some practical economic considerations to consider include the following:

- Would new faculty have to be hired, new equipment purchased, or library resources expanded?
- Would existing faculty have to be retrained? (See Chapter Nine, this volume.)
- Would current departmental relationships be changed in significant ways if faculty were asked to devote more time to the new program?
- What new or expanded relationships would be necessary with other institutions?
- What are the fiscal requirements to get the program started, sustain it, and ensure its long-term viability?
- Would it be necessary to reallocate major resources away from already determined college priorities?

College presidents also face a third major concern: the prospect of little or no support from traditionalists among campus constituents who envision already scarce resources being diverted from well-established institutional goals. However, the shrinking of traditional revenue bases has forced many outright opponents of career-related programs to alter their views. The result is that many practical courses and job-centered majors have been added to the curriculum. The discussion surfaces anew when such a collection of course offerings coalesces into a program that threatens to become permanent.

To determine whether or not a career program should be added, the president must guide the institution through a process of matching the proposed career program against the stated or commonly accepted aims and objectives of the institution. In this process the college or university will address the philosophical and practical considerations that must be weighed in reaching a decision to stop or proceed with a career program.

Problems of Mission Review

Two problems come to the forefront when conducting a review of the impact of the proposed career program on the institution's mission,

its stated philosophical underpinning. Those aims and purposes statements that exist in college catalogues and usually in the hearts and minds
of most faculty tend to include more references to knowledge, understanding, and belief (for example, knowledge of the principles of mathematics,
understanding of the roots of Western civilization, belief in the rule of
law) than to skills (for example, ability to program a computer). Even
though many of the courses already taught may emphasize skills as well
as understanding, a problem seems to arise when a program appears to
emphasize the latter over the former (that is, skills for job placement over
knowledge for lifelong enrichment. The belief that a liberal arts education
prepares its graduates for *any* occupation may be central to the mission of
the institution. How will adding a program that prepares students for a
specific occupation affect the broader liberal arts mission? How does the
mission statement reflect a belief in the liberal arts and in specific career
preparation? (For further discussion, see Chapter Ten, this volume.)

It is also important to note that there is probably not even
unanimity on the big picture within the campus community at any given
moment. If the college is not presently living up to its mission statement,
the debate is as much over whether to move further away or to attempt to
move back to original goals. A very important discussion may well be
opened up in the institution by the very practical matter of having to
reach a decision about a new program. At stake may be the image of the
institution, a precious commodity. Sensitivity to this must be balanced by
the courage to explore and willingness to take the calculated risk.

Three Basic Questions

When a college begins to consider a new career program, it must
ask itself three basic questions.

Is there a need for the program? There are two sides to this question.
Does the college need the program to enhance certain defined goals? These
may be institutional goals; the college may want to broaden its offerings.
Or the goals may be economic: the desire to draw more students. Or is the
college responding to a need in the community? There may be a need for
a four-year nursing program to support local hospitals. A successful program addition will be an attempt to meet either internal or external needs
and preferably both.

How and when does the determination of need take place? The
initial request may come from the outside; a representative of local industry may come to the president, or new equipment may provide opportunities for expanded program use. The gathering of pertinent data is essential
and should include information about (1) identifiable regional needs not
being met at present, (2) other similar programs offered in the area and
their enrollment and cost figures, (3) demographic data on students, and
(4) national and local employment trends. With this information the pres-

ident, who is the logical focal point for discussion in the earliest stages, should have support, at least in principle, from his or her major constituencies to continue the fact finding. The information received from these queries must be convincing to the president if he or she is to gain the widespread acceptance and support necessary in the adoption process. If the need is established, the second question must be asked.

Does the proposed program conform to the stated mission of the college? If the college already provides preprofessional courses of study (and most do) and if premedicine or prelaw or business administration can be used as examples, then some degree of credibility exists and the president can build on precedent. The task of convincing faculty, whose support will determine the fate of the proposed program, may be easier if some legitimacy has been established and there is no threat that the new program will be at odds with the basic liberal arts mission. A faculty that has never included any vocational or professional courses in its curriculum requires an entirely different approach, and a much longer period of debate will be necessary to advance interest in a career program. The new career program must be justified on academic grounds. Faculty must be convinced that the subjects to be introduced represent a worthy body of knowledge, are academically respectable, and will be taught by teachers with some evidence of scholarship. The need for academic acceptance is formidable.

Most college or university mission statements emphasize goals such as development of the whole person, importance of spiritual growth, acquisition of communications skills, understanding of world cultures, and the ability to think critically. Any career program or course of study could be designed to incorporate some or many of the above time-honored attributes of a liberal arts education. There is a temptation to think that nearly everything (especially when large economic rewards are possible) can be presented in a manner that is palatable to trustees, faculty, alumni, prospective students, and parents. However, faculty endorsement of the new program is crucial since they will implement it. Reasons why faculty might be favorably disposed to a new career program can range from recognition of the economic realities to the excitement of being part of a pioneering effort that enhances the stature of the college.

Can the institution afford the program? It is when one moves from the philosophical acceptance by institutional parties to a consideration of the implications for resource allocation and the impact on existing organizational structures (such as academic departments) that the road to final approval becomes rockier and filled with potholes of potential disaster. At this point the third question—can we afford it?—presents the greatest problem. In almost every case a bottom-line decision makes the difference. Start-up costs for people and equipment, questions of short-term versus long-term benefits, prospects of sustaining the program on its own if initial funding is from outside the college, chances of cost-sharing within and outside the college, probability of increased endowment, and the potential for donor support all enter into the final financial consideration. Even if the general philosophical tests of compatibility with institutional mission as described above have been met, revenue projections must reveal a strong base for success or the matter should be dropped altogether. If a new program is not affordable within current budget constraints, the discussions should end. If, however, the program appears to be philosophically and economically feasible, the discussions move to the next stage, that of mission review.

Mission Review: Philosophical Considerations

Four items must be considered and consensus reached regarding the effect of the new program on the college mission.

First, an additional career program might alter public perception of the college. Whether or not the new career program passes the philosophical mission test may be immaterial. Trustees, alumni, and parents may see the new direction as too innovative or judge it to be working at cross purposes with their understanding of the college's goals. The pure liberal arts college might be seen by some to be abandoning its sacred strengths to embrace a nontraditional program. Although this may not be the case at all, it is important to remember that the power of perception should never be underestimated. A president must endeavor to find out where key individuals stand, both intellectually and emotionally. The choice to proceed should prove less risky if a majority of college constituents yearn for a new image or see change as mandatory for regaining institutional momentum. Otherwise, more time will need to be spent aligning the new program's goals with the already existing purposes of the institution.

Second, current program offerings might have to be revised and new priorities established. Is the college willing to drop an undergraduate major, eliminate a graduate program, combine undergraduate departments, or assign faculty new teaching assignments so that the new career field might become part of the curriculum and have adequate academic respect? If the strengths of the new venture are apparent enough to silence most critics, reallocation of dollars may not prove to be an Achilles heel. If current programs will not be affected in a detrimental way or if a glaring institutional weakness is being eliminated, the merits of proceeding receive a great boost. Should neither of the above conditions exist, a lack of faculty support can be anticipated by those who will have to give up something (a course, a faculty member) so that the new program can commence. It is most important at this juncture for the president to be able to offer a positive sign to the affected faculty by providing appropriate avenues for input to ensure that all points of view are heard or that there is compensation in the form of new opportunities or responsibilities.

Third, the administration must be prepared to present in specific terms what outcomes it expects. The president will be expected to be more detailed about advantages than is probably possible in order to gain whole-hearted support within the academic community; he or she will also be forced to be present for committee review insights about the pitfalls. The president should plan to establish program review guidelines at the outset and provide for data collection to support or deny initial promises of increased enrollment or cost savings.

Fourth, the rationale for the new program will have to be explained to every constituency in understandable terms. The president will need to answer questions and allay fears as well as garner support. It will take an enormous amount of time and much of this time will be spent clearing up misconceptions and planting the seeds for new concepts of the college and its mission. The program may well rise or fall on the public persuasiveness of the president.

Mission Review: Practical Considerations

Some of the basic questions in mission review raised in the introductory section will surface again at this point. Why is the college contemplating the addition of a new career program? Will it bring in substantial numbers of new students, meet a visible regional need, or put the institution well ahead of its competitors for years to come? A good starting point for seeking the answers is the origin of the new career program. Did the impetus for considering the new program come from the trustees, the president, the faculty, the admissions office, the local chamber of commerce, the business community, the local hospital, an accreditation report, a statewide planning group in higher education, or an outside consultant? Any or all of these sources will be able to present compelling cases for or against the program and advise a president that he or she is either missing a good thing or leading the college down the path to ruin. The president must decide when to proceed with assignments for mission review and whom to consult.

The first specific review will need to be fiscal. Assuming the college has already decided that the program will be economically feasible, the question will then be the method of financing. Common pitfalls a president may encounter in the fiscal review include underestimating the time and cost of starting the program, underestimating the necessary phase in adjustments required, relying too much on soft money, being unrealistic in calculating long-term institutional costs, inability to gauge acceptance if a major reallocation of current funds is imperative, and allowing personal bias to interfere with assessment of the program's worth. Although economic and philosophical discussions are usually wide ranging and unstructured within the campus community, the actual process of mission review should follow a fairly strict format.

Usually (and wisely) the information-gathering tasks are assigned to existing committees or offices. (See Chapter Four, this volume.) Planning officers, institutional research staff, long-range planning committees, priorities committees, or other special advisory bodies that already deal with questions of aims and objectives of the college should be called on to review the program and make recommendations. Outside experts, such as consultants with established reputations or professional accrediting personnel (when new degree requirements are involved), may prove indispensable, especially if the president or members of the committee are not well versed in the career area under discussion. This will not be construed as a sign of weakness but rather that leadership wants the best available help to make the correct decision. (See Chapter Six, this volume).

The approval process begins as the curriculum committee of the college reviews the data and prepares a recommendation to the faculty. Positive action by both the initial reviewing body and the curriculum committee creates a favorable climate for deliberation by the full faculty. A positive response by the entire faculty or its representative equivalent is then transmitted to the appropriate academic affairs committee of the board of trustees, where a formal document is framed for presentation for full board endorsement. Although time consuming, successful use of this process provides as much of a presidential mandate as one can hope for and ensures the president of a base of support.

This process remains essentially the same regardless of the number or type of program additions. Most colleges are capable of considering only one or, at most, a few major program additions at one time. As a rule only a single-career program is considered if the field is new to the campus as a whole. The learning time can be longer or shorter but should be determined by the time necessary to reach broad consensus.

The process will vary somewhat with the size and type of institution. At small, private liberal arts colleges where missions are restrictive, the mission review process can be expected to be lengthy, since more vested interests have to be considered. The consequences of actions are more visible in the academic community and often in the town where the college is located. Church-related or denominational colleges as well as those with unique existing programs are less likely to adopt new career programs, since they already cater to a particular clientele, and thus the benefits of change may be less obvious. Large private colleges may have more flexibility or funds for innovation.

On the other hand, large public colleges or universities may face strict requirements mandated by state education departments or boards of regents that determine which programs can be considered. It is not uncommon to find limits on the number of particular programs that can be offered within a state system.

There are other external factors that influence the course of program review besides size and type of institution. Geographical location, economic conditions of the region, and existing cooperative relationships among colleges and/or businesses can affect any of the above procedures. Political realities also have a way of intruding.

Summary

Mission review of new career programs is not a neat and orderly process. However, when a new program is considered, there is no avoiding questions of need, mission compatibility, and money. Answers to these questions must run along positive lines for leadership to begin formal mission review with confidence.

The mission review process and its ingredients are clear but exceptions to the rule can be expected to be the norm. The process cannot be divorced from public perception and institutional politics. Perhaps next to the quest for funds, mission review is a president's most important business. Peck (1983, p. 39), in discussing leadership in small colleges, states: "These institutions were created out of a mission and they continue because of a mission. It is the mission which filters opportunities and ultimately determines destiny."

Reference

Peck, R. D. *Future Focusing*. Washington, D.C.: Council of Independent Colleges, 1983.

Allen P. Splete is former vice-president for academic planning and special projects at St. Lawrence University and former president of Westminster College. Currently, he is president of the Council of Independent Colleges.

Having a planning model, identifying a planning officer, gathering the necessary planning data, conducting a feasibility study, and understanding the institution's program approval process are key steps in deciding on a new career program.

Establishing the Planning Process for Selecting Appropriate Career Programs

Philip C. Winstead

Colleges should proceed with caution as they select the proper career programs to add to their curricula. They should base their decision on thorough and comprehensive institutional planning. Although colleges should respond to the genuine needs of their constituents, they cannot be all things to all people or simply respond to the whims of the market. They should add only those programs that support the institutional mission, goals and objectives, and those for which resources are available.

Although administrative imperatives play an important role, faculty should also be involved in the basic decision of what curricula to adopt. The administration usually determines overall program needs; the curriculum for the program, however, normally requires the approval of faculty. Early involvement of the faculty in the planning process is important to ensure curricular approval and institution-wide support of the program. This joint effort creates a balance between the authority of the administration as it determines the need for a specific career program and the authority of the faculty as it determines specific curricular offerings. At both the administrative and faculty levels, good decisions should always be based on reliable information and sound planning.

M.A.F. Rehnke (ed.). *Creating Career Programs in a Liberal Arts Context.*
New Directions for Higher Education, no. 57. San Francisco: Jossey-Bass, Spring 1987.

29

A good planning process begins with a recognized planning structure on campus. Whether or not there is a formal planning/institutional research office is not important. The planning officer can be an administrator or faculty member with responsibility for planning given on an *ad hoc* or temporary basis. It is important to note that the office or person charged with the planning function does not actually do the planning but provides the necessary data to coordinate the planning effort. The actual planning should be done by line officers and faculty if the program is to be implemented effectively. Very rarely is a program—a career program or any other type of institutional program—effective if those responsible for implementing the program are not centrally involved in the decision to initiate the program.

The remainder of this chapter describes a generalized planning model that is compatible with planning processes in most colleges and universities. This umbrella model emphasizes needs assessment, future considerations, institutional mission and scope, specific program planning, resource allocations, and staff support. The model is followed by a discussion of the institutional research function in this planning/decision-making structure, and the outline of a very detailed feasibility study format. The chapter concludes with discussion of topics such as available data sources, planning/decision-making support needs, and the institutional approval process.

A Planning Model

Although there is no one planning model suitable for all types of program planning, Green and Winstead (1975) note that most of the basic planning models useful in program expansion contain the following steps:
- Clarification of purpose, goals, and objectives
- Identification of opportunities
- Analysis of capabilities
- Determination of priorities
- Outlines of specific proposed programs
- Identification of future developments that will have a major impact on performance or results
- Allocation of essential resources
- Acceptance and support of key people who are involved or affected.

These steps or components, which are continuous and interactive, compose the basic flow of systematic or comprehensive program planning. Although all aspects of this general planning model are important for planning career programs, three stand out.

Needs Assessment and Capability Analysis Component. One procedure that can be adapted for needs assessment is a SWOTs analysis.

SWOTs is an acronym for a self-appraisal technique that has been used by colleges and universities to examine their Strengths, Weaknesses, Opportunities, and Threats. As a result of such appraisal, institutional programs can be formulated that maximize strengths, minimize weaknesses, take advantage of opportunities, or diminish threats.

An opportunity is something within the environment representing a need that (if within the mission and scope of the institution) clearly invites a positive programming response from the institution. A threat is a pending peril within the environment that, if not responded to, will be detrimental to the institution's future growth and development. This type of planning analysis can help identify possible career programs and determine whether or not it is feasible to undertake them.

Identification of Future Developments that Will Impact Performance or Results. This component relies on the recent influence of strategic planning concepts on traditional institutional planning techniques. The biggest difference between traditional planning and strategic planning is that strategic planning gives explicit recognition to the college's or university's outside environment, with specific emphasis placed on the institution's strategic advantage in meeting the contingencies found in the environment.

Of particular import for developing career programs is the fact that environmental scanning emerged in the early 1980s as one of the key elements in the evaluation process (Morrison, Renfro, and Boucher, 1983). Environmental scanning monitors emerging issues that pose threats or provide opportunities for the institution, such as the need for possible career programs.

Allocation of Essential Resources. Although hopefully the long-term potential of the proposed career program is to enhance the institutional budget, this is seldom true over the short term. There are usually start-up costs that if not adequately funded can jeopardize the overall success of the program. The institution must be willing, on potential alone, to provide the essential resources that will give the proposed program a fair chance to succeed.

Needs assessment and capability analysis, identification of future developments, and the allocation of essential resources are the steps that make the process realistic in terms of need, relevance, and commitment.

Outlining Specific Proposed Programs. This is important as a way to identify program elements and the resources required to carry out the activities. Otherwise decisions are likely to be made without adequate knowledge of the real costs, financial and human. The program outlines should be of sufficient detail to make decision makers fully aware of all of the implications associated with instituting a new area of activity. Such types of analyses called for are essential if appropriate priorities are to be established.

Acceptance and Support of Key People. Very few imposed programs are successful. A sense of ownership and pride in the proposed program is extremely important. The planning process should include elements designed to foster this commitment from the key people involved.

Conducting a Feasibility Study

If the institution has an office of institutional research, this office should perform the tasks of gathering and analyzing data. If there is no such office, a special task force can gather the information needed to support the feasibility study. Institutional research provides the research designs, measurement methods, statistical techniques, and other tools of systematic inquiry needed to make research-based decisions. Institutional researchers conduct applied research, interpret research results, and prepare research reports designed to aid decision makers in dealing with program planning questions.

With these overall planning elements in mind, planners can use the age-old trip analogy to make the transition from the suggested planning model to an organized structure for conducting a feasibility study that determines the efficacy of adding a specific career program. For instance, when planning a trip, these questions are appropriate: Where are you? Where do you want to go? How do you want to go? When do you want to go? Who is going with you? What will it cost? How do you know when you get there? Although these questions may appear almost too simple, the data necessary to respond adequately to them can provide a thorough and complete planning analysis structure for decision-making purposes. Also, the feasibility study requires a more detailed level of specificity than that provided by the general steps of the planning model.

Where Are You? Planners need to examine carefully the mission or purpose of the institution, the environment within which the college or university is operating, the competition the school is facing with regard to the program under consideration, and the institution's basic capabilities to perform in the proposed area. Questions related to mission or purpose include:

- What is the purpose of the institution?
- What are its traditional services?
- Who are the normal constituents receiving these services?
- How is the institution unique?
- What is the history of the institution in responding to perceived needs, especially as they relate to career programs?

Questions related to environment and competition include:

- What are the most important internal and external forces that will significantly affect the institution's ability to carry out the proposed program?

- What is the status of the economic, business, social, political, and educational environment for the nation, region, and the individual institution?
- Which of these environmental factors will aid or impede the proposed program?
- Who are the institution's competitors?
- How are they likely to respond or adapt in response to a new program?

Questions related to basic capabilities include:

- What unique skills, technologies, or facilities are needed for the proposed program?
- What facilities are available for the program?
- Are the leadership and initiative available for a new effort, especially in regard to the proposed career program?

This first part of the feasibility study defines the nature of the institution and the scope and purpose of the program and provides pertinent data on important environmental and competitive factors.

Where Do You Want to Go? This question makes assumptions about the circumstances that surround the proposed program and states specific goals and objectives. The assumptions are careful estimates of the important probable developments over which the institution has no significant control but which will have a major impact on performance or results. Assumptions can be divided into two categories: broad assumptions about the world in which we live and assumptions specifically applicable to the institution and the proposed new program. The first category might include economic, business, sociopolitical, and educational assumptions. The second category might include assumptions in the first category that relate specifically to the future nature of the institution, its environment, and its capabilities.

Establishing goals that provide a general sense of direction and are supported by measurable objectives is essential to any realistic feasibility study. For an objective to be measurable, it should include the six elements of time, outcome, performer, action, accomplishment level, and measurement. Time is the period in which the objective is to be accomplished. Outcome is the expected accomplishment. The performer is the one responsible for accomplishing the objective. Action is what is to be done to accomplish the objective. The accomplishment level is the acceptable level of performance. Measurement is how the accomplishment is to be determined.

How Do You Want to Go? This question deals with policies and procedures and describes the proposed program in as much detail as possible. Policies are broad statements of general intent indicating what is permitted or expected. A procedure is a more specific instruction that outlines how to do it. A program is a course of action that enables the institution to achieve the objectives within the framework of policy guidelines. It is not possible to understand the full implications of the career program under investigation unless one understands the basic policies and procedures that control the institution's current and future activities.

Two factors must be clearly identified in this step: (1) areas where policy and procedure guidance is needed to perform effectively, and (2) areas where existing policies and procedures are likely to prevent the best possible performance. To identify these areas and determine how the proposed program will fit into the overall planning, one must be thoroughly familiar with the program being proposed. Program description is the heart of the feasibility study. A decision cannot be made without a full knowledge of the proposed program to as specific a level of detail as practical. The program is the instrument that transforms a theoretical plan into a viable course of action.

When Do You Want to Go? This question outlines priorities and schedules. Such analysis helps determine and control who does what and what comes first. Since there are never enough resources to do everything that needs to be done, priorities must be set, an order of accomplishment must be established, and a corresponding timetable must be developed.

Who Is Going with You? This question covers human resources and the staffing of the proposed program. This portion of the study focuses attention on all aspects of personnel administration, manpower planning, and personnel relations related to the proposed new career program. More important, it promotes concentration on future problems and opportunities of organization and delegation that will be created by the introduction of a new program on campus. (For further discussion, see Chapter Nine and Chapter Ten in this volume.)

What Will It Cost? This question projects financial and physical resources, that is, the budgeting of the program. The cost estimates associated with the proposed program are the most important data in the entire study. Planning can become a snare and a delusion unless adequate resources (human and financial) are provided to carry out the proposed program. This section of the study should include information about the institutional and program budgets as well as how they impact each other.

Few colleges can afford programs that result in a financial drain on the institution's fiscal resources. Planners must ask questions about income and cost. For example,

- How much revenue will the new program generate?
- Will the additional program be cost effective?
- Will the revenue generated by the new program displace revenue now resulting from other existing programs?
- Will there be start-up costs? If so, how much?
- Will there be additional space needs?
- What about the need for additional library resources?

- Will there be a negative impact on existing overhead and maintenance costs?
- What is the probable life of the program?
- Will there be a need for specialized fixed equipment that could not be used for other purposes if the new program turned out to be short lived?
- Are there student financial aid implications? Will there need to be special financial aid considerations in the early years of the program in order to get the enrollment to the desired level?
- If new faculty are required from outside the present staff, will their salary requirements be compatible with those of the existing faculty in other fields?

The list of financially related questions is extensive, but all must be considered in depth if a wise decision is to be made. (For further discussion, see Chapter Three, Chapter Five, and Chapter Six in this volume.)

How Do You Know When You Get There? This question describes both a formative and summative evaluation process. The two types of evaluation will enable those who determine whether or not to proceed with the program to tell after a period of time if the program is meeting the agreed-on objectives. There should be measures outlined and evaluation procedures discussed as a part of the feasibility study to determine quantitatively and qualitatively how well the program does. (For further discussion, see Chapter Seven, this volume.)

A thorough report dealing with the issues raised by the trip analogy questions should provide the basic facts that decision makers need to make a sound judgment. Such a report developed under the rubric of the overall planning model suggested should allow decision makers to decide if a specific career program ought to be added to the curriculum.

Data Sources

There is a truism in the planning field that the quality of one's plans and decisions cannot consistently rise above the quality of the information on which the plans and decisions are based. The good planner will locate the appropriate information, analyze and consolidate it, and, most important, give the data in usable form to the appropriate decision maker.

The data needed for effective planning come from both external and institutional sources. For example, the federal government has numerous studies and reports depicting economic and demographic trends. An excellent place to start is with the *Occupational Outlook Handbook* published by the Bureau of Labor Statistics (United States Department of Labor, 441 G Street N.W., Washington, D.C. 20212). This publication describes various career opportunities, the qualificatons needed, the competencies required, and the training needed. The United States Department of Labor also publishes the *Handbook of Labor Statistics,* which is helpful for career planning purposes. The National Bureau of Economic Research (1050 Massachusetts Avenue, Cambridge, Mass. 02138) studies cycles of employment in the United States. Another source of career-related pamphlets, reports, and statistics is the Department of Health and Human Services (200 Independence Avenue S.W., Washington, D.C. 20201).

At the state level there are data available on manpower supply and demand, demographic trends, and educational statistics; the office title varies from state to state. In addition, individual states publish the results of different task forces on labor-related topics. Competent private sources continually produce marketing surveys of various kinds.

Internally, enrollment trends, faculty supply-and-demand data, institutional income, and expenditure patterns can all be studied as these factors relate to societal needs for institutions, programs, and other educational services. The National Center for Education Statistics (555 New Jersey Avenue, N.W., Washington, D.C. 20203) provides a wealth of data and projections on educational matters. All of these basic data sources should be used in developing the feasibility study.

Other Issues

Any time a major change is being considered in a complex organization such as an institution of higher education, those doing the planning must not only ask what is true but also what *else* is true. Any organizational change has a unique way of affecting other aspects of the institution. Will the new program attract new students to the campus or will the students be drawn from existing programs and therefore weaken them? Will an influx of new students change the desired student body mix with regard to age, sex, housing, minorities, and so on? Is present staffing adequate or will additional staff be needed? These and other questions must be addressed to ensure that solving one problem does not unintentionally create additional problems.

Support Needs

Introducing a new career program into the curriculum will have to be a joint institutional effort that will necessarily affect many aspects of the college community. Adequate preparation must be undertaken in a number of related campus offices. For example, efforts must be coordinated with the career planning and placement office so that mechanisms are in place to assist graduates in locating appropriate job opportunities. A necessary corollary may be an expanded internship program or some other type of work-study opportunities.

One area often overlooked is the need for proper academic advising. Faculty, especially in liberal arts institutions, are often not as competent as they should be in advising students who are interested in specific vocation or career fields. Thus educating faculty about adequate advising becomes part of planning a new career program.

Approval Process

The institutional approval process involving faculty and administration is a key element from the very beginning of new program development. For public institutions the approval process is even broader; they will probably need to submit any proposed new program to a state coordinating board or other state agency that concerns itself with institutional mission, levels of academic work, and program duplication. More and more private institutions also find that they are a part of a statewide master plan for postsecondary education. Thus on-campus planning must take into account the submission and approval cycles of state agencies. In all cases the overall planning, feasibility study, internal approval, and external approval must be accomplished within a time frame that allows for the proper phasing in of the new program, taking into account program publicity, staffing, curriculum development, student recruitment, space allocations, and the myriad administrative details needed for effective implementation.

Summary

Of the changing demands placed on institutions of higher education in recent years, none has been more crucial than the increased emphasis on job-related education. There is a public concern for demonstrable practical benefits from postsecondary education. The public is also concerned about quality and efficiency within institutions of higher education. Thus there is a growing need for sound planning and wise decision making as colleges and universities undertake the important task of curriculum development for new career programs.

References

Anthony, W. P. "Effective Strategic Planning in Nonprofit Organizations." *The Nonprofit World Report,* 1984, *2* (4), 12–16.
Green, E. J., and Winstead, P. C. "Systematic Institutional Planning." *Educational Technology,* 1975, *15* (7), 33–35.
Morrison, J. L., Renfro, W. L., and Boucher, W. I. (eds.). *Applying Methods and Techniques of Futures Research.* New Directions for Institutional Research, no. 39. San Francisco: Jossey-Bass, 1983.

Philip C. Winstead is coordinator of institutional planning and research, professor of education, and coordinator of faculty development programs at Furman University, Greenville, South Carolina.

Changing the programmatic structure of a higher education institution requires a keen sensitivity to the legal rights of students and faculty and the attendant risks.

Legal Issues: Identification and Management

David J. Figuli, R. Claire Guthrie, Andrew L. Abrams

Most institutions of higher education have 70 percent or more of their operational budget committed to personnel, with a substantial portion of that amount supporting legally enforceable tenure or tenure-like employment relationships. New programs require a significant infusion of funds to support personnel, capital equipment, program administrative support, institutional overhead, marketing, and a wide variety of start-up costs. Since these funds will most likely come from an internal reallocation, existing personnel and programs will be impacted. Also, adjustments will be needed in the contracts of the new career program faculty. Career programs will place less emphasis on terminal degrees and scholarship and more on professional competency. Career faculty will bring with them salary and benefit demands reflecting the professional marketplace. Accommodations will need to be made in faculty employment practices, such as rank promotion and tenure standards, evaluative standards and evidence, work-load definitions, salary distribution methodologies, and outside activity regulations. Students attracted to career programs will generally have a greater consumer sophistication and demand greater accountability for course and program objectives and preparation for professional licensure and certification.

All of these changes will require careful attention to existing and developing legal rights. Administrators should scrutinize three areas of

M.A.F. Rehnke (ed.). *Creating Career Programs in a Liberal Arts Context.*
New Directions for Higher Education, no. 57. San Francisco: Jossey-Bass, Spring 1987.

career program impact: faculty contracts, student contracts, and programmatic decisions.

Faculty Contract Issues

The introduction of career programs affects faculty contract rights in two ways. First, the reallocation of resources may eliminate existing faculty either as a result of eliminating or curtailing a program or as a result of reallocating funding from one area to another. Second, the modified role of career program faculty will usually necessitate a revision of existing faculty employment policies.

The outplacement of faculty requires a recognition of legally significant distinctions. There are three traditional faculty contract types: term, probationary/tenure-track, and tenure/continuous. Three techniques affecting faculty reductions are (1) ending continuing employment rights based on a legally sufficient cause, (2) inducing a bilateral agreement to modify the continuing employment rights of the faculty member, and (3) allowing the contract rights to expire, such as providing required notice of nonrenewal in the case of a probationary or tenure-track employee.

The contract type determines which techniques are appropriate. To terminate a faculty contract during its term, the institution must establish a legally sufficient cause, provide constitutional due process (in the case of public institutions) (*Allen* v. *Lewis-Clark State College*, 1983; *Leland* v. *Heywood*, 1982), and follow contractual due process (in the case of public and private institutions). Term contracts, commonly used for unranked faculty positions, exist for a stated period of time and automatically terminate at the end of the period. If the reduction decision does not shorten the identified term, then, generally, no continuing employment rights are affected. If, however, the reduction decision affects its stated term, procedural and substantive legal obligations must be satisfied (*Board of Regents* v. *Roth*, 1972; *Russell* v. *Harrison*, 1984). A similar analysis applies to probationary or tenure-track contracts. The difference between probationary and term contracts is the notice requirement for nonrenewal. If a faculty member with a probationary contract is terminated before the initial contract term or the notice period, then procedural and substantive rights accrue (*Bellak* v. *Franconia College*, 1978). If the contract term and the notice are allowed to run their course, no continuing employment rights are invaded. For a tenured faculty member a legally sufficient cause and appropriate process must attend the termination. (American Association . . . , 1984; Hendrickson and Lee, 1983).

Legally sufficient cause for invasive action, that is, action that seeks to set aside continuing employment rights, is limited to specific causes such as incompetence, or factual circumstances such as financial exigency. Whether a higher education institution can terminate faculty with continuing employment rights due to a change in program depends on whether the option for termination has been established expressly or implicitly in the faculty contract. To determine such intent one should review the pertinent employment policies of the institution such as the faculty appointment contract, the faculty handbook, a policy manual, or other official policy statements. American higher education institutions have commonly adopted variations of policy suggestions promulgated by higher education associations. Each has recommended some level of program discontinuance as a legitimate cause for termination of faculty continuing employment rights. (American Association . . . , 1984; Furnis, 1976). If an institutional policy exists one should carefully consider the terminology employed, since a variety of concepts may be incorporated within the circumstantial category of program discontinuance. If institutional policies do not speak to the termination of faculty for programmatic reasons, the courts will often imply such exceptions to continuing employment rights based on the custom within higher education, such as those statements of common understanding promulgated by higher education associations. The courts frequently have been willing to recognize the right of the institution to terminate continuing employment rights of faculty for "programmatic" reasons (*Jiminez* v. *Almodovar*, 1981; *Browzin* v. *Catholic University of America*, 1975).

An invasive termination must follow appropriate procedures, including adhering to institutional policies (*Piacitelli* v. *Southern Utah State College*, 1981). Even where no institutional procedures exist, a hearing opportunity may prevent a lawsuit. Public institutions must also account for constitutional due-process requirements. Essentially, the process prescribed by the Fourteenth Amendment of the U.S. Constitution and parallel state constitution provisions (as explained in *Johnson* v. *Board of Regents of the University of Wisconsin System*, 1974) requires that the affected faculty member be given a written statement of the basis for the initial decision to lay off and the manner in which it was arrived at, a description of the information and data relied on, and an opportunity to be heard in response to the decision. Constitutional procedures are required to ensure that the termination decision is rationally related to a legitimate cause (*Chung* v. *Park*, 1975). These procedures also provide an audit of institutional judgments and actions.

Noninvasive methods of effecting faculty reductions are many and varied. The most common is to not renew untenured faculty after fulfilling all contract obligations. Among others, Kreinin (1982) proposed severance pay, temporary reductions from full-time to part-time assignment with full retirement credit, reassignment from contracting to expanding units with retraining support, reduction from fiscal- to academic-year appointments without a fully proportional reduction in salary, and partial or full early retirements to help reduce the staff at Michigan State University in

1981. More recently, Mortimer, Bagshaw, and Masland (1986) have iden-
tifed four discrete opportunities for institutions to reduce expenditures
and reallocate personnel by controlling replacements for vacancies; reducing the number of new tenure-track and tenure appointments made; reducing the rate of tenure accretions by quotas, extended probationary periods,
suspension of the "up-or-out rule," tougher tenure standards; and increasing the attrition rate of tenured faculty by early retirement incentives,
posttenure review, and reassignment.

New Faculty Contracts

The different orientation of career program faculty requires new
institutional employment policies, which should be clearly stated in the
faculty handbooks and incorporated by reference into the individual faculty appointment contracts.

To add career program faculty one should begin with a staffing
plan that defines the number of faculty needed on a short- and long-term
basis; the type of contract relationship; the rank, promotion, and tenure
standards; performance and evaluation criteria and standards; and a compensation plan (Figuli, 1985). Career faculty may have nontenure-track
appointments until the program is economically and academically viable.
Long-term staffing may include tenure-track and nontenure-track positions to allow for cyclical adjustments in enrollment caused by market
demand alterations while maintaining a stable core of senior faculty.

Student Issues

Breach of Contract Claims. The legal rights of students must be
factored into any decision to restructure or eliminate their academic program. Also, institutions implementing new programs must be careful to
avoid creating expectations that later may prove difficult to meet. Students
may have a legal right to money damages if representations made about a
new program prove to be false.

Courts and commentators agree that the student-university relationship is contractual in nature. The enrollment contract draws life and
form from a variety of sources, including school catalogues, bulletins,
circulars, internal rules, and other oral and written statements that give
rise to reasonable expectations of the institution's obligations. In its strict-
est terms the enrollment contract includes the implicit understanding that
if a student enrolls in a particular program and meets the academic and
financial obligations imposed by the institution, the student is entitled to
a degree at the completion of the program. Thus a student may have a
legally enforceable expectation that the program will continue to exist
throughout the period ordinarily required for completion. This principle
is intrinstically difficult to reconcile with institutional needs for flexibility.

It is clear that a school's written material (usually the catalogue) is the greatest source of legal problems for the school and gives rise to breach-of-contract claims. The contract between institution and student generally is implied rather than made explicit from these materials. Thus to limit an institution's exposure, it is necessary to begin by defining carefully in any information disseminated to its students the scope of an institution's obligations. Further, while the courts generally have allowed institutions great latitude in developing and subsequently modifying written commitments, the existence of unqualified obligations places an institution in the defensive position of having to demonstrate why its own writings are modified by extrinsic factors such as custom, usage, financial necessity, or impossibility of performance.

Additional Legal Considerations. A student who has a breach-of-contract claim because an old program is being phased out or a new program is not as advertised may also have a tort claim for misrepresentation or fraud, particularly if it can be argued there was an intent to deceive on the part of the institution. State consumer laws also may protect students recruited into new programs. Further, students at state universities may have a right to due process before their enrollment contract can be terminated by a change in a program.

Federal law also is relevant in establishing and marketing new programs for the following reasons:

1. Tax-exempt schools must advertise a nondiscriminatory admissions policy.
2. Any program restricted to a certain age group may violate the Age Discrimination Act of 1975.
3. Student aid rules prescribe certain student-consumer standards that must be met.
4. Proprietary school's advertisements must comply with Federal Trade Commission rules.

Policy Recommendations. The following general policy guidelines should be helpful in minimizing exposure to student suits when changing or adding programs:

1. All documents disseminated by the institution should be scrutinized for accuracy, consistency, and possible expectations created.
2. An institution should not promise in any document to continue a course or institutional program indefinitely. Instead it should state clearly that the school retains the absolute right to modify its programs at any time.
3. Where the basis for programmatic change is financial, the institution should be prepared to produce convincing evidence of fiscal problems in order to survive judicial scrutiny.
4. Whenever feasible an institution should phase in program changes rather than terminate a program immediately. As long as a pro-

gram exists accreditation should be maintained and the quality of the program kept consistent with generally accepted standards of appropriate educational organizations.

5. Close attention should also be paid to state and federal statutory requirements.

Programmatic Issues

Many new academic or career programs must meet licensing and accreditation requirements to be viable. This is of particular significance to private institutions and public institutions operating out of their states of residence. In addition, internships (or externships) often incorporated in career programs may raise special liability problems for the sponsoring institution.

Licensing. Self-regulation of academic programs through voluntary accreditation often is supplemented now by state or local licensing rules that apply more frequently to out-of-state and degree programs. These rules have been challenged in the courts, usually unsuccessfully.

A number of general legal concepts can be gleaned from the case law. Educational institutions have no inherent or constitutional right to confer degrees; instead, degree conferral involves business conduct and, as such, is a privilege subject to regulation. Due to the valid governmental interest in protecting student consumers, licensure provisions will likely be upheld as long as they are applied in a nondiscriminatory fashion. Although the courts approve of regional and specialized accreditation, because of the voluntry nature and the perceived powerlessness of the accrediting bodies to prevent the award of substandard or fraudulent degrees, the courts have had no difficulty finding that governmental entities may have a legitimate interest in setting and enforcing minimum degree standards through licensure.

This is true regardless of whether professional or nonprofessional degrees are involved. The critical emphasis remains on the degree. The fact that an institution formally awards its degrees outside the licensing jurisdiction will not insulate it from regulatory control; the primary focus is on where the educational activity actually takes place. At the same time, state and local licensure laws often permit an institution to offer *nondegree* courses without first obtaining a license, since it is the public reliance features of the degree that make it subject to valid regulation.

Institutions contemplating program initiatives both in and, particularly, out of state should be scrupulous in complying with the licensing rules of the states where the education activity will take place. The applicant institution should realize that, because of the judicial reluctance to intervene, the decision by the accrediting/licensing body may be final.

Liability Issues. Both public and private institutions must examine closely the potential exposure to liability in tort that may arise from operating successfully licensed and accredited programs. Although an institution generally has no duty to protect its students from injuries sustained in unsupervised activities (*Bradshaw* v. *Rawlings*, 1980), institutions are susceptible to potential liability in institution-sponsored academic programs. Courts will hold institutions to a higher degree of care in ensuring the safety of their students engaged in curricular, as opposed to private, activities. This increased duty is attributable to the fact that curricular activities are more closely aligned with the academic mission of the school and thus are more properly the subject of institutional supervision and control.

When these general liability principles are considered in the context of career programs, the potential risks to the institution become apparent. In the case of those internships that are located on campus or with close contact, are under academic supervision, and provide course credit, the institution bears the same responsibility to its student interns as to its other students engaged in curricular pursuits. This should not pose a monumental problem to the institution; present means of risk management should suffice to control exposure to liability in these programs. Unfortunately, this is not necessarily the case when experiential externships are involved.

The first difficulty in assessing potential liability arising out of an externship is in determining the precise nature of the externship program. These programs vary greatly. A school may serve only as a clearinghouse for matching up students and sponsors, or the school may supervise its students at on-site training locations. The greater the supervisory role the institution plays in the externship process, the greater the likelihood that a court will conclude the school has assumed a duty to protect its student externs from risk of harm.

Some commentators suggest that because an institution could be held liable for actions taken by students or harm occurring to students while under the supervision of an outside agency, the institution should visit the proposed work environment. By visiting the site and purporting to inspect its safety, however, the institution may be creating a duty and thus potential liability for itself where none previously existed. If such an inspection is realistically unlikely to permit the institution to evaluate and mitigate potential risks, the benefits of the review would not appear to outweigh the increased liability that exposure engendered.

A reasonable alternative to on-site inspections is to inform student externs of the respective responsibilities of the student and school and to seek a waiver of liability. By clearly articulating its nonsupervisory role in the externship process and the specific responsibility of the student versus the school to assess the safety of the proposed work environment, the school can undercut any expectation by the student that the school has undertaken to guarantee the safety of the outside program.

The institution also should carefully examine both the risks posed by the externship program and the risks covered by any existing or contemplated liability insurance policy. A serious cost-benefit analysis of any insurance policy should be conducted due to the substantial expense of insurance. Even then, liability insurance will only supplement, not supplant, other methods of protection.

In addition to questions of liability to students enrolled in externship programs, there is an issue of potential liability of the school to the sponsor firm for misconduct by the student. The institution should clearly state in both written and oral communications with the sponsor that the school makes no representations regàrding the student's health or fitness for the particular activity and instead only communicates its student's interest in the sponsor's given area of work. Moreover, the institution should endeavor to negotiate an agreement with the sponsor that ensures that the sponsor assumes and indemnifies the institution for any risk arising out of the student's activities while the student is under the sponsor's supervision and control.

Policy Recommendations. To minimize the liability and maintain quality career programs, institutions should consider implementing the following recommendations:

1. Publications and communications to both student and sponsor should clearly state the limited role of the school as coordinator, not supervisor. All conduct should be consistent with this limited role.

2. The student should be given and acknowledge receipt of a clear statement of his or her responsibilities in any externship program, including the evaluation of the nature and safety of the proposed work. This document should also contain a general waiver and release of liability.

3. If the institution is aware of any specific risks of employment, these should be communicated to the student; however, the institution should avoid any appearance that it is guaranteeing student safety.

4. Whenever economically feasible, liability insurance coverage for actions by and against the student extern should be obtained. In addition, an agreement should be negotiated with the externship sponsor that ensures that the sponsor accepts responsibility for its negligence in supervising externs.

5. In the event of injury to student or sponsor the institution should avoid any explicit or implicit admission of liability and should immediately turn the claim over to the institution's lawyers.

Summary

The introduction of career programs on campus ushers in programmatic, fiscal, and personnel dynamics that will likely be unsettling to existing student and faculty contract rights. Also, career programs by their nature expose an institution to more liability risks that do more traditional programs. The academic manager is advised to incorporate the identification and analysis of legal considerations as a part of the planning for and the management of these programs.

References

Allen v. *Lewis-Clark State College.* Ida. 447, 670 P.2d 854 (Ida. 1983).
American Association of University Professors. *AAUP Policy Documents and Reports.* Washington, D.C.: American Association of University Professors, September, 1984.
Bellak v. *Franconia College.* 386 A. 2d 1266 (N.H. 1978).
Board of Regents v. *Roth.* 408 U.S. 564 (1972).
Bradshaw v. *Rawlings.* 612 F.2d 135 (3d Cir. 1979), *cert. denied,* 446 U.S. 909 (1980).
Browzin v. *Catholic University of America.* 527 F.2d 843 (D.C. Cir. 1975).
Chung v. *Park.* 514 F.2d 382 (3rd Cir. 1975).
Figuli, D. J. "Employee Management Imperatives." *The Journal of the College and University Personnel Association,* 1985, *36* (2), 32–36.
Furnis, W. T. "The 1976 AAUP Retrenchment Policy." *Educational Record,* 1976, *57* (3), 33–39.
Hendrickson, R. M., and Lee, B. A. *Academic Employment and Retrenchment: Judicial Review and Administrative Action.* ASHE-ERIC/Higher Education Research Report, no. 8. Washington, D.C.: American Association for Higher Education, 1983.
Jiminez v. *Almodovar.* 650 F.2d 363 (1st Cir. 1981).
Johnson v. *Board of Regents of the University of Wisconsin System.* 377 F.Supp. 227 (W.D. Wis. 1974), *aff.d,* 510 F.2d 975 (7th Cir. 1975).
Kreinin, M. E. "Preserving Tenure Commitments in Hard Times: The Michigan State Experience." *Academe,* March–April 1986, pp. 37–42.
Leland v. *Heywood.* 643 F.2d 578 (Mont. 1982).
Mortimer, K., Bagshaw, M., and Masland, A. "Academic Staffing: Be Flexible and Fair." *AGB Reports,* March–April 1986, pp. 29–31.
Piacitelli v. *Southern Utah State College.* 636 P. 2d 1063 (Utah 1981).
Russell v. *Harrison.* 736 F.2d 283 (5th Cir. 1984).

David J. Figuli is president of Higher Education Group, Inc., Denver, Colorado, and head of the Education Law Department of Wickens, Herzer, & Panza, P.C., a multistate law firm.

R. Claire Guthrie is deputy attorney general of the Commonwealth of Virginia. Her responsibilities include providing legal advice to the state's public colleges and universities. She has practiced in the field of higher education law since 1974 and has taught a higher education law seminar at the University of Virginia School of Law.

Andrew L. Abrams is vice-president of legal affairs at the College of Charleston and also assistant professor of business.

Accreditation is a voluntary process attesting to educational quality; when linked by legislation to the certification or licensure of professionals, it can become mandatory.

Accreditation, Certification, and Licensure

Marjorie Peace Lenn

To assist colleges and universities considering the addition of a career program, this chapter outlines accrediting procedures and legislated linkages and describes the costs related to the accrediting process. The literature claims accreditation as the primary communal and voluntary means of quality assessment and enhancement in American higher education. It is true that accreditation is an internalized activity that is a direct, self-regulatory creation of the academic and professional education communities and is administered by nongovernmental associations of institutions, programs, and professionals in particular fields. However, one can take issue with the extent to which it is a voluntary exercise of the higher education community. A significant portion of the voluntary nature of accreditation was forfeited in 1952 when Congress enacted the Serviceman's Readjustment Act, tying accreditation to eligibility for federal funds. This act was followed by others (typically Manpower Acts) at the federal or state level that tied professional licensure and, in a few cases, certification to graduation from an accredited program.

Institutional and Specialized Accreditation

Colleges and universities receive authorization by a state to operate and institutional accreditation by a regional or national accrediting body

M.A.F. Rehnke (ed.). *Creating Career Programs in a Liberal Arts Context.*
New Directions for Higher Education, no. 57. San Francisco: Jossey-Bass, Spring 1987.

attesting to the educational quality of the institution as a whole. In complex institutions several programs (such as law, medicine, engineering, and theology) may also be accredited by specialized accrediting bodies. These bodies require that an institution be accredited by a recognized institutional accrediting body before any of its programs can be considered for accredited status. There are fourteen institutional accrediting bodies recognized by the Council on Postsecondary Accreditation (COPA) and the U.S. Department of Education. Nine of these are postsecondary commissions of the six regional associations, as follows:

- Commission on Higher Education/Middle States Association of Colleges and Schools
- Commission on Higher Education/New England Association of Schools and Colleges
- Commission on Vocational, Technical, and Career Institutions/ New England Association of Schools and Colleges
- Commission on Institutions of Higher Education/North Central Association of Colleges and Schools
- Commission on Colleges/Northwest Association of Schools and Colleges
- Commission on Colleges/Southern Association of Colleges and Schools
- Commission on Occupational Education Institutions/Southern Association of Colleges and Schools
- Accrediting Commission for Community and Junior Colleges/ Western Association of Schools and Colleges
- Accrediting Commission for Senior Colleges and Universities/ Western Association of Schools and Colleges.

Five institutional accrediting bodies operate nationally and accredit particular types of institutions.

- Commission on Accrediting/American Association of Bible Colleges
- Accrediting Commission/Association of Independent Colleges and Schools
- Accrediting Commission/National Home Study Council
- Commission on Accrediting/Association of Theological Schools in the United States and Canada
- Accrediting Commission/National Association of Trade and Technical Schools.

Institutional (or specialized) accreditation is not automatically extended when an institution expands its offerings in any significant manner on or off campus. It is the responsibility of the institution to inform the institutional accrediting body when a substantive change, such as the creation of a career program, is being seriously considered or developed (COPA, 1985). And it is the obligation of the accrediting body to ensure the quality and integrity of all programs of the institution, wherever located (COPA, 1983). Of central concern are issues of program integrity, administrative and academic control, quality assurance, availability of resources, and supervisory accountability.

If it is determined that the program is separately accreditable, evaluation of the educational activity is the responsibility of the region in which the program is taught (COPA, 1983). In cases where institutions have created distance-learning programs delivered via telecommunications, accrediting bodies will know whether the institution has appropriate authorization to operate in any state in which they wish to offer instruction (COPA and State Higher . . . , 1984). (For a more in-depth look at legal considerations, please refer to Chapter Five, this volume.)

Whereas institutional accreditation attests to the educational quality of the institution as a whole, specialized accreditation focuses on the quality of educational programs generally accepted as preparation for entry levels for a particular profession or occupation. There are thirty-six specialized accrediting bodies recognized by the Council on Postsecondary Accreditation (COPA). Recognition attests to the need for accreditation in a particular area and the ability of an accrediting body to meet specified standards related to accrediting policies and practices. Those bodies that accredit at least in part at the undergraduate level are listed in Figure 1. The U.S. Department of Education recognizes thirty-two of COPA's thirty-six bodies plus eleven others. Five of these eleven are on the undergraduate level and are as follows:

- National Accrediting Commission of Cosmetology Arts and Sciences
- National Association of Schools of Dance
- American Board of Funeral Service Education
- National Association of Schools of Theatre
- Commission on Animal Technician Activities and Training, American Veterinary Medical Association

Of the four COPA-recognized bodies not recognized by the U.S. Department of Education, three conduct accrediting activities at the undergraduate level. They are the American Council for Construction Education, the American Home Economics Association, and the Council on Rehabilitation Education.

Relationship of Accreditation to Certification and Licensure

Accreditation, certification, and licensure originated as processes whose purposes and objectives were separate and distinct. Over the past decades, however, operational relationships among them have often become so closely linked that legitimate and essential distinctions have been blurred or ignored.

Definition of Terms. For the purposes of this chapter, the following definitions are stipulated for the processes:

1. *Accreditation* is a communal, self-regulatory process by which nongovernmental voluntary associations recognize educational institutions or programs that have been found to meet or exceed stated criteria of educational quality and assist in the further improvement of the institutions or programs.

2. *Certification* is the process by which a nongovernmental association grants recognition to an individual who has met certain predetermined qualifications specified by the association and who voluntarily seeks such recognition.

3. *Licensure* is the process by which an agency of government grants permission to persons meeting predetermined qualifications to engage in a given occupation and/or use a particular title (National Commission on Accrediting, 1971, p. ii).

Accreditation and certification are nongovernmental and licensure is governmental. Certification and licensure evaluate and attest to individual achievement and competence; accreditation evaluates and attests to institutional or programmatic quality.

However, legislative action for the express purpose of protecting the public has in several cases inextricably tied the licensure and, in some cases, certification of an individual to graduation from an accredited program. Twelve of the accrediting bodies recognized by COPA and with accrediting activities at the undergraduate level are so affected. (Two of the twelve bodies are part of the Committee on Allied Health Education and Accreditation (CAHEA) of the American Medical Association, an umbrella organization for sixteen allied health accreditation programs. COPA recognizes CAHEA as a single unit.)

Figures 1 and 2 were developed primarily to show where linkages do and do not exist between specialized accreditation and certification and licensure. Figure 1 lists those specialized accrediting bodies where linkages do not exist. Figure 2 lists those where there are linkages. Only those accrediting bodies that accredit, at least in part at the undergraduate level, are listed. On both charts the first column indicates the profession or occupation, and the appropriate accrediting body and where it can be contacted. The second column denotes the accrediting scope recognized by COPA for each body. Figure 2 has a third and fourth column. Although there are multiple legal considerations to be taken into account when creating a career program, it is important for this particular purpose to note in the third column when the eligibility requirements of an accrediting body require a particular legal status prior to being eligible for accreditation. The fourth column indicates those cases in which certification or licensure is tied to graduation from an accredited program. Any more specific information concerning the accreditation standards and procedures of an accrediting body can be obtained directly from the body of interest.

Costs of Educational Quality

Academic administrators are well aware that programs that are equipment dependent (health related or laboratory programs, for example) or programs that offer salaries higher than the institutional norm in order to retain faculty (such as business or engineering) are more expensive to the institution than programs without these needs. Because the basic costs of a program are so dependent on the specific nature of the profession or field being taught, it is appropriate that the respective professional body be consulted. Because accreditation standards are tied to all aspects of a career program, it is impossible to distinguish between costs of accreditation for status reasons and costs related to educational quality. Accreditation attests to educational quality, but the quality is relative to the specific objectives of a program, the administrative or institutional circumstances in which the program operates, and the human and physical resources available to the program.

Assessing Process Costs. It is possible, however, to address some of the particular costs of the accreditation process itself. This process begins with a self-study, is followed by a site visit of peers representing the accrediting body, and concludes with a final accrediting decision made by that accrediting body. Another crucial part of the accreditng process, as the functions of accreditation extend beyond assessment to include enhancement activities, is its internalization in the planning processes of the program and institution.

Recent attempts to identify the costs of the accreditation process beyond the recorded transaction of fees have identified at least three kinds of costs that should be included in an accurate assessment (Parks, 1982; Kennedy, Moore, and Thibadoux, 1985).

1. The determination of an applicable institutional overhead figure that gives a realistic estimate of expenses
2. Fiscal outlays for services and materials utilized, including
   a. Printing or photocopying
   b. Postage
   c. Computer time
3. Payroll for time expended by
   a. Administrators
   b. Faculty
   c. Consultants
   d. Clerical staff

Accrediting activities, whether in preparation for a self-study or in the planning mode between site visits, are labor intensive. However, with

Figure 1. Recognized Accrediting Bodies at the Undergraduate Level in Which There Is Not a Linkage Between Accreditation and Certification or Licensure

COPA Recognized Accrediting Bodies	Recognized Accrediting Scope
Allied Health—See Below	
Architecture National Architectural Accrediting Board 1735 New York Avenue, NW Washington, D.C. 20006 Tel. (202) 783-2007	First professional degree programs.
Art and Design Commission on Accreditation National Association of Schools of Art and Design 11250 Roger Bacon Dr., Suite 5 Reston, Virginia 22090 Tel. (703) 437-0700	Institutions and units within institutions that offer degree programs in art, design, and art/design related disciplines; also non-degree-granting institutions.
Business Administration—Management and Accounting Accreditation Council American Assembly of Collegiate Schools of Business 605 Old Ballas Road, Suite 220 St. Louis, Missouri 63141 Tel. (314) 872-8481	Bachelor's and master's degree programs in administration, management, and accounting.
Construction Education Accreditation Committee American Council for Construction Education 1015 15th Street, NW, Suite 700 Washington, DC 20005 Tel. (202) 347-5875 or (301) 593-7284	Baccalaureate programs in construction, construction science, construction management, and construction technology.

Dietetics
Commission on Accreditation
The American Dietetic Association
Div. of Education and Research
430 North Michigan Avenue
Chicago, Illinois 60611
Tel. (312) 280-5093

Coordinated baccalaureate programs in dietetics and post-baccalaureate internship programs.

Home Economics
Council for Professional Development
American Home Economics Association
Office of Professional Education
2010 Massachusetts Avenue, NW
Washington, DC 20036
Tel. (202) 862-8355

Units offering baccalaureate degree programs.

Interior Design
Committee on Accreditation
Foundation for Interior Design Education Research
322 Eighth Avenue, Suite 1501
New York, New York 10001
Tel. (212) 929-8366

Programs from the junior college through the graduate level in interior design and interior design and interior architecture.

Journalism
Accrediting Council on Education in Journalism
and Mass Communication
School of Journalism
Stauffer Flint Hall
University of Kansas
Lawrence, Kansas 66045
Tel. (913) 864-3973

Units and programs leading to undergraduate and graduate (master's) degrees in journalism and mass communications.

Figure 1. (*continued*)

COPA Recognized Accrediting Bodies	Recognized Accrediting Scope
Librarianship Committee on Accreditation American Library Association 50 East Huron Street Chicago, Illinois 60611 Tel. (312) 944-7680	First professional degree programs for librarianship.
Medical Assistant and Medical Laboratory Technician Board of Commissioners Accrediting Bureau of Health Education Schools Oak Manor Offices 29089 U.S. 20 West Elkhart, Indiana 46514 Tel. (219) 293-0124	Diploma, certificate, and associate degree programs for medical assistants and medical laboratory technicians.
Music Commissions on Undergraduate Studies, Graduate Studies, Community/Junior Colleges, and Non-Degree-Granting Institutions National Association of Schools of Music 11250 Roger Bacon Drive, Suite 5 Reston, Virginia 22090 Tel. (703) 437-0700	Institutions and units within institutions that offer degree programs in music and music-related disciplines; also non-degree-granting institutions.
Rabbinical and Talmudic Education Accreditation Commission Association of Advanced Rabbinical and Talmudic Schools 175 Fifth Avenue, Rm. 711 New York, New York 10010 Tel. (212) 477-0950	Rabbinical and Talmudic schools that offer rabbinical degrees, ordination, and appropriate undergraduate and graduate degrees in the field of rabbinical and Talmudic education.

Allied Health

COPA recognizes the Committee on Allied Health Education and Accreditation (CAHEA) of the American Medical Association as an umbrella agency for 16 review committees, which represent 39 professional organizations collaborating in the accreditation of programs in the undergraduate areas of allied health listed below. Allied health agencies outside of CAHEA are listed individually by discipline in Figures 1 and 2. Inquiries concerning accreditation of the following programs should be directed to:

Division of Allied Health Education and Accreditation
American Medical Association
535 North Dearborn Street
Chicago, Illinois 60610
Tel. (312) 645-4660

Programs:
Specialist in Blood Bank Technology, Cytotechnologist, Diagnostic Medical Sonographer, Electroencephalographic Technologist, Emergency Medical Technician-Paramedic, Histrologic Technician/Technologist, Medical Laboratory Technician (Associate Degree), Medical Laboratory Technician (Certificate), and Medical Technologist, Medical Assistant, Medical Record Administrator and Medical Record Technician, Nuclear Medicine Technologist, Ophthalmic Medical Assistant, Perfusionist, Assistant to the Primary Care Physician and Surgeon's Assistant, Radiation Therapy Technologist and Radiographer, and Surgical Technologist.

Figure 2. Recognized Accrediting Bodies at the Undergraduate Level in Which There Is a Linkage Between Accreditation and Certification or Licensure

COPA Recognized Accrediting Bodies	Recognized Accrediting Scope	Eligibility Requirements for Accreditation Involving Prior Legal Status*	Licensure or Certification Tied to Graduating from an Accredited Program
Allied Health—See Below			
Dentistry and Dental Auxiliary Commission on Dental Accreditation American Dental Association 211 E. Chicago Ave. Chicago, IL 60611 Tel. (312) 440-2708	First professional programs in dental education; advanced specialty programs; general practice residency; and degree and certificate programs in dental auxiliary education.		Dentists and dental hygienists (except dental hygienists in Alabama) must be graduates of an accredited program to be eligible for state licensure.
Engineering Engineering Accreditation Commission Technology Accreditation Commission Accreditation Board for Engineering and Technology 345 E. 47th St. New York, NY 10017 Tel. (212) 705-7685	Professional engineering programs at the basic (baccalaureate) and advanced (master's) level as determined by each institution; baccalaureate programs in engineering technology; and two-year (associate degree) programs in engineering technology.		State licensing authorities, either by specific statute or by long-standing practice, generally recognize ABET-accredited engineering programs for full education credit toward satisfying State Professional Engineer Licensure requirements.
Forestry Committee on Accreditation Society of American Foresters 5400 Grosvenor Lane	First professional degree programs, baccalaureate or higher, in forestry.		Twelve states currently have registration and/or licensing laws affecting foresters (AL,

Bethesda, MD 20814
Tel. (301) 897-8720

AR, CA, GA, ME, MD, MI, MS, NC, OK, SC, WV). In some states graduation from an accredited program is a requirement.

Landscape Architecture
Landscape Architectural Accrediting Board
American Society of Landscape Architects
1733 Connecticut Ave., NW
Washington, D.C. 20009
Tel. (202) 466-7730

First professional degree programs.

Most state licensure statutes require graduation from an accredited or recognized program for licensing as a landscape architect.

Nursing
Boards of Review for Baccalaureate and Higher Degree, Associate Degree, Diploma, and Practical Nursing Programs
National League for Nursing
10 Columbus Circle
New York, NY 10019
Tel. (212) 582-1022

Associate, baccalaureate, and higher degree programs; also diploma and practical nurse programs.

Program approval without qualification by the state board of nursing. (*Note:* State boards of nursing do not have jurisdiction over master's degree programs or programs admitting previously licensed registered nurses.)

Optometry
Council on Optometric Education
American Optometric Association
243 N. Lindbergh Blvd.
St. Louis, MI 63141
Tel. (314) 991-4100

Professional programs in optometry and optometric technology.

Legal authorization by appropriate state agency to confer the Doctor of Optometry degree.

Most states require graduation from an accredited program for licensure.

Figure 2. (*continued*)

COPA Recognized Accrediting Bodies	Recognized Accrediting Scope	Eligibility Requirements for Accreditation Involving Prior Legal Status*	Licensure or Certification Tied to Graduating from an Accredited Program
Pharmacy American Council on Pharmaceutical Education 311 W. Superior St., Ste. 512 Chicago, IL 60610 Tel. (312) 664-3575	First professional degree programs (baccalaureate or doctoral) in pharmacy.		Statutory or regulatory requirements in all states include graduation from an accredited program as a prerequisite for licensure.
Physical Therapy Commission on Accreditation in Education American Physical Therapy Association Transpotomac Plaza 1111 N. Fairfax St. Alexandria, VA 22314 Tel. (703) 684-2782	First professional degree programs for the physical therapist, and programs for the physical therapy assistant.		Graduation from an accredited program is required for licensure of physical therapists in all states and for physical therapist assistants in 28 states.
Social Work Commission on Accreditation Council on Social Work Education Division of Education Standards and Accreditation 1744 R St., NW Washington, D.C. 20036 Tel. (202) 667-2300	Baccalaureate and master's degree programs in social work.		35 states require degrees from accredited programs for licensure or certification.

Teacher Education
National Council for
  Accreditation of Teacher
  Education
1919 Pennsylvania Ave., NW,
  Ste. 202
Washington, D.C. 20006
Tel. (202) 466-7496

Baccalaureate and graduate
degree programs for the
preparation of teachers and
other professional school
personnel.

Approval by State Board of
Education at the degree levels
and in the categories for
which accreditation is sought.

Allied Health
Of the 16 accrediting committees described at the end of Figure 1, the following two reflect a linkage with certification or licensure:
Occupational Therapist—Certification by professional association requires graduation from accredited program.
Respiratory Therapist and Respiratory Therapy Technician—Graduation from an accredited program is required to sit for the
licensing examination.

Note: All specialized accreditation requires prior institutional accreditation by a recognized agency, which in turn requires prior state authorization
for the institution to operate.

the occasional exception of an external consultant hired to help in an initial accreditation process, there usually are not increases in the staff or payroll to accommodate this need. Typically, administrators exchange some portion of their responsibilities for the task of writing the report or coordinating the campus part of the process, and faculty find that some portion of their usual committee time is used to address the task.

Accrediting Body Fees. A direct cost of accreditation is found in the fees assessed a program or institution by the accrediting body. These fees cover expenses related to training sessions for visiting team members, site visits, meetings related to the review process, administrative and consultative services, and publications. Their totals are broad ranging, reflecting the diversity of services provided by the various accrediting bodies. There are four types of fees, each representing different points in the accrediting process, namely, (1) the initial processing fee, (2) the annual fee, (3) the fee related to the campus site visit (when the visit or some portion of the arrangements for the visit are administered directly by the accrediting body), and (4) the reaccreditation fee. (Many accrediting bodies collect an annual fee in lieu of a reaccreditation fee.) Not all accrediting bodies collect all four types of fees. Some have an initial processing fee and operate solely from fees collected at the time of the site visit. Most operate on fees generated from the initial processing and campus site-visit phases of the process in combination with an annual fee.

Several factors can help offset fees, such as volunteerism, subsidization, and decentralization. The majority of labor provided in the peer review is volunteered. In real terms another institution is paying for the time of a peer to conduct an evaluation on your campus. Once your career program is in place, you will likely be given the opportunity to reciprocate. In addition, the costs of accreditation are often subsidized by the professional association to which the accrediting activity is related. As association income is typically derived from the dues of its membership; the entire profession, including its practitioners and educators, is contributing to the accrediting process. Finally, many accrediting bodies delegate the responsibility for site-visit arrangements to the campus so that there is reasonable local control over expenditures. The combination of these factors helps considerably in reducing the costs of the process.

Summary

In the process of creating a career program, the institution must ask three questions of itself relating to issues of accreditation, certification, and licensure. First, how will the addition of a career program affect the current institutional accreditation of the campus? Second, is there a recognized, specialized accrediting activity for the particular career program being considered? And third, if there is an accrediting activity for the career area, what linkages exist between program accreditation and certification or licensure in the field?

Sources of Information

Council on Postsecondary Accreditation, One Dupont Circle N.W., Suite 305, Washington, D.C. 20036 (202) 452-1433
U.S. Department of Education, Division of Eligibility and Agency Evaluation, Accrediting Agency Evaluation Branch, Higher Education Management Services, GSA Regional Office Building, Mail Stop 3316, 7th and D Streets S.W., Washington, D.C. 20202 (202) 245-9703

References

Council on Postsecondary Accreditation (COPA). "Off-Campus Credit Programs." Policy statement of the Council on Postsecondary Accreditation, Washington, D.C., April 1983.
Council on Postsecondary Accreditation (COPA). "Rights and Responsibilities of Accrediting Bodies and Institutions in the Accrediting Process." Policy statement of the Council on Postsecondary Accreditation, Washington, D.C., April 1985.
Council on Postsecondary Accreditation (COPA) and State Higher Education Executive Officers. "Accreditation and Authorization of Distance Learning Through Telecommunications." Policy statement of the Council on Postsecondary Accreditation and the State Higher Education Executive Officers Association, Washington, D.C., October 1984.
Kennedy, V. C., Moore, F. I., and Thibadoux, G. M. "Determining the Costs of Self-Study for Accreditation: A Method and a Rationale." *Journal of Allied Health*, May 1985, pp. 175–182.
National Commission on Accrediting. *Study of the Accreditation of Allied Health Educational Programs*. Washington, D.C.: National Commission on Accrediting, 1971.
Parks, R. B. "Costs of Programmatic Accreditation for Allied Health Education in the CAHEA System: 1980." Paper prepared for the American Medical Association, Chicago, February 1982.

Marjorie Peace Lenn has seventeen years of experience in higher education administration, several of these as a division head at the Amherst campus of the University of Massachusetts. She is currently director of professional services at the Council on Postsecondary Accreditation in Washington, D.C.

Assessment is crucial to the assurance of quality in the award of academic credentials and for feedback to improve curricula and instruction.

Assessment: Providing Quality Assurance for Students, Programs, and Career Guidance

John Harris

Increasingly, the businesses and industries in which graduates seek jobs view quality assurance as crucial to their survival. Inevitably, they expect it of higher education. Just as today's buyers demand cars that run economically with minimal maintenance, employers expect college graduates to speak coherently, write clearly, compute accurately, think logically, and demonstrate in-depth knowledge and skills in a special field.

Quality assurance is more than increasing the probability that graduates are competent. It is also the means of systematically improving a program in terms of its consequences.

In language more related to education, there must be some means of comparing "expectations" with "actual achievements" of graduates. Too often an educational program is structured around a preset educational theory on the assumption that if the theory is reflected in the program, appropriate results will follow. Educators rarely turn the empirical "microscope" on their own area. But in career education we must.

M.A.F. Rehnke (ed.). *Creating Career Programs in a Liberal Arts Context.*
New Directions for Higher Education, no. 57. San Francisco: Jossey-Bass, Spring 1987.

Build In Assessment

To make a career education program an instructional system, assessment must be a key component from the beginning. If it is an afterthought, it will not mean much except as a means of paying lip service to evaluation, possibly for some accrediting body. If one expects to optimally manage program resources—students, faculty, and instructional technologies—a system of assessing program outcomes is essential. Assessment provides information on actual consequences; it allows comparison of the *is's* with the *oughts*. Rarely are we able to design perfect programs before they begin to operate. An emphasis on assessment is an honest admission that most of us need to correct programs.

Much outcomes assessments is done using outside, commercially produced tests. Whether intended or not, the implication is: "We don't trust the judgment of the faculty in the award of course grades, so students will take this outside test to determine if their faculty awarded grades are justified." Understandably, faculty usually have little sustained interest in such approaches to assessment. To avoid this implied criticism when designing a new program in career education, why not build the courses around the crucial expected abilities? Have an assessment procedure for each course or program component that can stand on its own, so that colleagues, students, and employers will say, "If someone measures up to the way they are assessed in those courses in that program, they are competent."

Assessment provides empirical information for two purposes: (1) accountability (Are graduates as competent as their degrees indicate?) and (2) feedback (Is the instructional program as effective, efficient, and accepted as it could be?).

Instructional System Components

In this chapter a systems approach to curriculum and instruction is assumed. In general an instructional system includes the components that follow:

1. *Objectives.* Objectives are stated in terms of expected student performances or products so that they may be assessed by two or more examiners against definite standards. A general education skill every student might be expected to demonstrate is expository writing reflecting logical organization and correct grammar and usage. A given college might also expect students to be able to explain in their words the economic and financial terms commonly used in the business sections of daily newspapers. At the senior level students might be expected to demonstrate integrated and practical knowledge of their major field through papers or projects. For example, information science students at one col-

lege completed a project that analyzed the information needs of a dentist's office and identified commercially available software and hardware to meet those needs and in another project designed a personal computer data-based system for an individual investor to record transactions in mutual funds.

2. *Curricula.* Content or information is selected as a means of achieving expected student performance or products.

3. *Instruction.* Learning activities are developed as a means of engaging the student with the curriculum in order to produce the desired outcomes.

4. *Assessment.* Assessment is any means that compares student achievement with instructional objectives.

5. *Feedback.* Feedback uses assessment information to determine (1) if the original objectives are appropriate and (2) if the curriculum and instruction yield the expected results with the most efficient use of student and teacher time and energies.

Descriptions of Graduates' Abilities

Once this commitment to assessment is made, the first task is to describe the graduate in terms of demonstrable knowledge and skill. Avoid descriptions such as

The graduate has had certain courses.

The graduate has been exposed to . . .

The graduate understands and appreciates . . .

A useful way to approach this task is to answer these two questions: (1) What would a graduate in this field be able to do that a generally able person without this particular education would not be able to do? and (2) What projects or tasks would distinguish entering from exiting students? Answer these questions with statements that contain verbs depicting performances or requiring products and specific levels of expected performances or products (minimize adjectives and adverbs).

Some examples of statements that describe specific tasks students may be asked to do to demonstrate expected abilities follow:

1. When presented with a list of incidents and statistics about discipline problems in an elementary school, write an imaginary letter to the local school board accurately representing the facts of the list using logical and correct grammar as judged by two or more independent readers.

2. When asked to lead a small group in a problem-solving exercise, demonstrate to two or more observers effectiveness in helping the group

68

state the problem objectively, enumerate alternative solutions, and describe a practical process for the selection of the most cost-effective solution.

Answers to these questions in the suggested way provide a foundation for developing a useful assessment system. These questions help faculty articulate the *unique* knowledge and skills associated with a given program.

At this point representatives of employers may contribute to defining the distinctive abilities of graduates. As committees are appointed to develop various career programs, employers should be included. They usually help balance educators' tendency to take the long view of student preparation. Educators may emphasize theory, but employers expect immediately useful skills. Both outsiders and faculty probably assume general literacy and math skill when in fact we need to be specific about both expectations.

Basic Assessment Procedures

One way to conduct assessment is to test students separately from the award of credit. In addition to taking regular tests within courses, a student is asked or required to take a comprehensive test covering his or her major field. A student completing his sophomore year may also take a battery of general education tests on such areas as writing, mathematics, science, and so on. In addition to ability tests, students or graduates may be asked to complete questionnaires inventorying such things as personal values, opinions of the institution, campus activities, and so forth. A widely used test of general education is ACT's College Outcome Measures Project (COMP). The College Board provides an essay test for use in colleges. Among a number of questionnaires for assessing student perceptions of the institution or their particular programs are the following:

- Institutional Goals Inventory (ETS)
- Small College Goals Inventory (ETS)
- Student Reactions to College (ETS)
- Program Self-Assessment Service—Faculty, Student, and Alumni Questionnaires (ETS)
- COMP Activity Inventory (ACT) (An inventory of student activities related to general education.)
- Adult Learner Needs Assessment Survey (ACT)
- Alumni Survey (ACT)
- Entering Student Survey (ACT)
- Student Opinion Survey (ACT).

The intent of these assessments is to determine the general competence of students as well as their typical attitudes and behaviors. Such testing provides proximate information to answer such questions as (1) What, if anything, is unique about our students or graduates? (2) Are our students growing in the desired direction? (3) Are our students and graduates satisfied with the services of this institution?

A one-time assessment of student abilities provides a statistical snapshot of a student body or graduating class at a given point. It cannot provide information to gauge change or infer cause. The best way to assess change is to test, or inventory, the same students at two points in their college careers (longitudinal assessment). A less accurate but quicker way to assess change is to test, or inventory, two comparable groups of students at different levels at the same time (cross-sectional assessment). For example, a sample of beginning freshmen and a sample of rising juniors might be tested on their writing abilities. If there is control for initial differences, a useful comparison of the average performance of the two groups can be made.

Before-and-after testing schemes can indicate change but not cause. Only a tightly controlled experiment isolates the possible effects of a given educational treatment as distinct from general maturation. For example, determining whether writing instruction actually contributes to the tested differences between freshmen and sophomores requires a second group similar in initial writing abilities, educational background, age, general aptitude, and other relevant variables and uninstructed in writing. The difficulty of this arrangement is obvious even for a major research effort and much more so for an individual institution.

One-time assessment strategies that yield statistical snapshots of students' and graduates' abilities and opinions help faculties spot strengths and weaknesses. For example, an analysis of senior psychology students' answers to a comprehensive test on psychology could indicate they are strong in history and systems and weak in measurement. Similarly, longitudinal and cross-sectional assessment strategies help a faculty determine the direction and amount of growth. Sometimes there are surprises: Writing and computation skills may decline after the end of the freshman year. Such findings could, for instance, spark interest in a writing-across-the-curriculum program.

Testing Problems

If an institution can get students to cooperate in taking tests not related to credit, it can use such tests to inspect itself. Institutions obviously do not use such tests as the basis for certifying competence; the regular course examinations are assumed to do this.

Over time, students and faculty come to perceive assessment strategies that are outside of or beyond the award of credit as extra burdens. Furthermore, students often do not do their best because the tests do not "count." They may even refuse to take the tests. To deal with this situation, some institutions require all students to take certain tests to graduate. In the case of general education tests, students may be required to make certain minimal scores to move from lower-division to upper-division status or to graduate. In both of these latter cases, there can be an issue of double jeopardy. That is, if a student has passed course tests, he or she may question taking other tests on the same content.

Building Assessment into Credit Systems

In contrast to these add-on strategies, stronger assessment procedures can be built into the credit-instructional system. Rather than adding a rising-junior writing test, a comprehensive writing test may be made a part of composition courses. Rather than administering a major-field examination to seniors separate from their regular senior courses, a senior comprehensive course may be developed around an assessment of seniors' knowledge of and skill in their major fields. A senior comprehensive course would include projects such as those done by the information science students described earlier.

Perhaps we could take a cue from Japanese industry. Any worker can stop the assembly line when products are not meeting specifications. Quality assurance becomes a responsibility of every worker. Quality must become the number one priority.

Developing Effective Assessments

There are several guides to follow in developing effective and respected assessments.

Externality. Some provision must be made to reference the assessment against some defined standard beyond the instructor's individual judgment. One way colleges try to do this is by publicizing grade distributions. Extreme percentages of either high or low grades are taken to indicate idiosyncratic grading. This approach guards against extreme or deviant grading behavior, yet it is insensitive to subject matter and instructional differences.

There are four provisions for externality that can greatly improve assessment.

1. *Explicit, public statements of expected student attainment.* Explicit statements of general education abilities such as those given earlier should be included in the general education requirements section in the institution's catalogue. Descriptions of senior papers and projects should be included with the description of each major in the section of the catalogue describing major course requirements.

2. *Explicit, public statements of assessment procedures.* For instance, writing samples judged by certain specified criteria can be used as standards.

3. *Use of one or more examiners in addition to the instructor.* In career education it would especially be helpful to use as examiners individuals who practice the respective specialties in the work world.

4. *Use of national, commercially available tests* (such as those listed in the basic assessment procedures in this chapter) *as part of a total assessment program.*

Relevance. Obviously, career education must help students acquire knowledge and skills beyond what are needed for entry. On the other hand, if graduates cannot perform when hired, the program loses credibility with employers and with graduates. To keep assessment relevant, establish a way to provide feedback into the assessment practices through recent graduates' and entry-level supervisors' opinions of graduates' on-the-job skills. Each department or the placement office might send a questionnaire to the employer of graduates within the first year of the graduate's employment. In the questionnaire the employer would be asked to assess the technical, communication, and interpersonal skills of the graduate. There is considerable advantage in having the respective departments directly involved in such surveys. The placement office could develop a common format with some common, across-the-institution questions, and each department could add unique questions.

Validity. Are the assessment procedures measuring what they are purported to measure? Do they correlate with other similar, respected measures? Do they correlate with relevant on-the-job performances?

Consistency. Do the assessment procedures yield reliable scores or ratings? Do ratings of student performance or products reflect variables other than the specific competency being assessed? When multiple raters are used, are their independent judgments similar? Is an individual rater consistent across cases and over time?

Security. Although students should know what knowledge and skills they are expected to demonstrate, they obviously should not know specific test items. This is handled in English universities by publishing the questions used the previous year to test candidates for degrees. Obviously, different but similar items are developed each year. This is a very practical way to help all candidates know the type of questions to expect.

Up to this point, two uses of assessment have been covered, namely, certification of competence and feedback of results on processes (curriculum, instruction, faculty, and admission). There is another major potential use of assessment for career education: student guidance.

Assessment for Student Guidance

A career means one's life work. It is generally assumed that the greater the congruence among an individual's values, interests, abilities, and type of work, the greater his or her chances for personal happiness and social contribution. Given these assumptions, assessment that helps the student understand himself or herself more objectively will help in choosing a life's work.

With the commitment to help each student make the best decisions about career comes the obligation to provide an assessment-counseling program from entry to exit. Beginning students should have the opportunity to consider a self-profile against a profile of the vocation they are considering. These profiles should include assessments of abilities as well as values, interests, and behavior patterns. There are several well-known inventories of interests that help individuals compare their interests to various occupations. Three of the most used are the Strong-Campbell Interest Inventory, Kuder Preference Record, and Holland Self-Directed Search.

American College Testing and Educational Test Service now offer comprehensive assessment programs to assist students in career choices. ACT's Discover and ETS's SIGI (System of Interactive Guidance and Information) are interactive, computer-based guidance programs. Although there are differences in these two programs, both inventory the self-assessments by students of their interests and abilities, provide students with relevant occupational information, and assist them in using this information in career planning.

When high school students take the ACT Assessment, they may also complete the Uni-ACT Interest Inventory. Given their responses to the Interest Inventory, the Student Profile Section of the ACT Assessment score report allows them to locate themselves on a Map of College Majors and a World-of-Work Map.

ACT also offers the Career Planning Program, which includes six ability measures, an experience inventory, an interest inventory, and a planning section. This program helps students integrate their tested abilities and inventoried experiences and interests in career planning.

Typically, campus counseling centers administer various personality inventories to persons seeking counseling. All students should be involved in a comprehensive guidance program that should include developing career-relevant profiles for each entering student. Then the student should be given the opportunity to discuss the implications of the profile with someone who can relate the profile of the student to his career possibilities. Ideally, the student should have the continuing opportunity to relate assessed course performance to career choices.

Mentor Program

A strong emphasis on assessment for certification of competence, feedback for program improvement, and student guidance makes a mentor system very desirable. A mentor is someone who combines the role of academic adviser, tutor, and guidance counselor. As soon as a student has decided on a given career education program, he or she should be assigned a mentor. The mentor guides the student to the exit competencies of a particular program and directs the student in the senior comprehensive.

Before the senior comprehensive the mentor has functioned not only as the typical academic adviser but also as the primary link of the student to his career field. The mentor's task is to shape the student in competence and understanding to be effective in a given career.

How does mentoring relate to assessment? The course examinations, general education skills tests, and aptitude and interest measurements of the students provide data for their ongoing conversations. The mentor becomes something of a craftsperson, using the assessment data to guide his or her work with the student. Assessment can therefore lead to a more humane as well as more effective way of producing graduates who are suited by attitude as well as skill to their chosen careers.

Summary

A commitment to assessment should be a part of a larger commitment: viewing the education program as an instructional system. Joseph Hammock has said that a good system is characterized by explicitness, comprehensiveness, and tentativeness. By tentativeness he means that an instructional system is never permanent; rather it is constantly being modified in terms of its consequences. It builds in a feedback loop and uses it for continuous improvement. Assessment provides the hard data for the feedback loop.

For the most part, college curricula have not been developed as instructional systems. In large measure they represent an amalgamation of the educational philosophies of past and present faculties. Career programs should be developed as instructional systems. If they are, strategies and instruments of assessing student performances and products will be developed early in the program's development. These strategies should be developed as soon as the exit abilities of graduates are defined and before the curricular and instructional patterns are established.

Reference

Hammock, J. Personal communication, University of Georgia, 1970–1972.

John Harris is professor of psychology and E. H. Ijams
Professor of Christian Education at David Lipscomb
College. He has written about, worked in, and consulted on
instructional development and assessment in numerous
colleges and universities. Most recently, he wrote one of six
commissioned papers for the AAHE-sponsored and Office
of Education–funded National Conference on Assessment in
Higher Education. He serves on the secretary of education's
National Advisory Committee on Accreditation and
Institutional Eligibility.

*Recruiting and retaining minorities and women students for
nontraditional careers remains a challenge for contemporary
educational planners, but with new program initiatives
designed for this population, this situation may change.*

Strategies for Recruiting and Retaining Minorities and Women in Nontraditional Programs

Carol J. Carter

During the past decade much has been written to document the changing
characteristics of students enrolled in American colleges and universities.
Racial minorities, older individuals, and women are emerging as the new
student, and demographic projections suggest that this trend will continue.
With the decline in the number of traditional-age students occupying
college and university classrooms, administrators of postsecondary institutions need to implement strategies to recruit and retain this new population. As educational planners initiate career programs, care must be
taken to recruit minorities and women who continue to be underrepresented in many of the high-paying careers and professions.

   This chapter reviews some key factors in developing programs for
minorities and women in nontraditional careers. Specifically, it will examine methods for attracting and retaining minorities and women in higher
education and will provide strategies to assist educational planners in
developing programs for this student group.

M.A.F. Rehnke (ed.). *Creating Career Programs in a Liberal Arts Context.*
New Directions for Higher Education, no. 57. San Francisco: Jossey-Bass, Spring 1987.

Institutional Responses to Minority Students

When blacks and other minorities arrived on predominately white campuses, many institutions were not ready for a heightened minority presence because they had virtually no experience from which to draw on. Efforts to retain minority students were generally relegated to special programs that were usually separated into two broad categories: academic and cultural programs.

Academic programs were established to assist academically underprepared students in overcoming scholastic deficiencies through developmental and remedial courses. An array of support services such as individual counseling, tutorial assistance, and course advising were often an integral part of these program initiatives.

Nonacademic programs were structured to facilitate social and cultural activities on campus. They were usually housed in a cultural center where students could meet and plan their events. These centers helped decrease the sense of alienation experienced by many students on campus and facilitated outreach by them into the larger community.

Two major criticisms have been leveled at the concept of special programs. First, too little data exist to assess the educational impact of the programs on students. Second, institutions were unable to identify effective features that benefit minority students.

Career Choices Among Minority Students

Research in the area of career development among minority groups is minimal. However, the available studies reveal that minority students who graduate from college are overrepresented in disciplines with the lowest pay and limited employment opportunities, namely, education and social sciences. They are underrepresented in nontraditional disciplines such as engineering, biological science, mathematics, and physical science.

Astin (1982) in his study on minorities in higher education and the distribution of various racial and ethnic groups finds that they prefer certain academic disciplines. The four minority groups (American Indians, blacks, Chicanos, and Puerto Ricans), he notes, avoid biological sciences, engineering, mathematics, and physical sciences.

Additional studies on nontraditional careers for this population identify strategies that may be helpful in recruiting prospective students to these professions. Dunteman and others (1979) found a relationship between socioeconomic status of black students, their choice of quantitative majors, and the educational aspirations of parents. The authors note that it is important to provide young people early academic training and encouragement to pursue nontraditional disciplines.

Trent (1984) observes that although the proportion of black students attending predominately black colleges has declined since the 1970s, the majority of black students earning degrees in mathematics and quantitative disciplines are graduating from black institutions.

Institutional Responses to Women Students

Unlike special programs created for minority students, academic programs designed for women were usually developed within an existing department such as English, history, or sociology. From these efforts many women's studies programs evolved. Women's studies was multidisciplinary, with many faculty members promoting the value of including the contributions of women within respective disciplines.

Support services were an extension of the nonacademic programs established for women. Activities were usually conducted at a women's center and ranged from providing personal counseling to conducting workshops on financial management and career planning.

Professional staff was hired to supervise and coordinate services for women. Ultimately, these centers emerged as advocacy sites where women sought institutional support for such issues as day care, increased hiring of women for faculty and administrative positions, and the endorsement of curricular change in various academic departments.

Career Choices of Women

Studies on career development theories do not fully explain the career patterns for women. Further, the majority of the studies were conducted on males with little consideration given to women. However, more recent analyses of career development reveal how society affects women's career-goal aspirations. Generally, women are not encouraged to compete openly with males. These social lessons are very effective, because as girls women internalize many of the values and expectations regarding career choices from a male-dominated society. Sandler and Hall (1982) in their study on the classroom climate and its impact on women noted that women also generally feel excluded and disregarded as serious students in the classroom setting.

Research on older or returning women students indicates that many of them are made to feel as if they have betrayed their family, friends, and relatives and must adopt new coping strategies to withstand the criticism if they major in certain academic disciplines. However, more recent studies on this group of women acknowledge that women become competent learners as they engage in formal education (Pappas and Loring, 1985; Holliday, 1985).

Research on black women and women of color in nontraditional careers is limited. One study of black female undergraduates majoring in mathematics, science, and engineering documents that students experienced a sense of alienation, personal isolation, and rejection by the instructors in the classroom (Scott and Hohrn, 1975). Other research points out that as black women achieve status and success, they demonstrate self-confidence, perform effectively in their respective careers, and maintain positive attitudes about encouraging other women to enter the fields (Epstein, 1973; Scott, 1977; Scott and Horhn, 1975). Despite the strides being made by women to pursue nontraditional careers, studies show that women of color continue to lag behind males and white females (Hodgkinson, 1985; Jackson, 1974).

Studies of career choices made by women reveal that such decisions are influenced by sex and occupational stereotyping and by the aspirations of both males and females. The expectation is that individuals will be attracted to those professions classified as gender appropriate (Terborg, 1977). Yet research shows that the final determinants of career choice appear to be prestige, nature of the work, and personal characteristics that affect occupational preferences (Anderson and others, 1984; Axelson, 1974; Kanter, 1975; Knudson, 1982).

Characteristics of Successful Women Students

Despite social barriers and gender distinctions, women are selecting nontraditional careers. More recent studies indicate some of the factors that may assist women in career choices. Kingdon and Sedlacek (1982) conducted a study to determine the differences between female students choosing traditional careers and those choosing nontraditional careers. The results indicated that those women who chose nontraditional careers (1) had a high achievement orientation, (2) appeared not to participate in sex role stereotyping, (3) developed better study skills, and (4) were encouraged to explore nontraditional interests.

In addition to identifying the characteristics of successful women students, the study also confirms the positive influence role models have on women in their pursuit of nontraditional careers.

Recommendations

Recommendations for retaining minorities and women in nontraditional career programs should be based on a comprehensive institutional assessment before the actual implementation of programs addressing the areas of administrative concerns, program initiatives, and support services.

Administrative Concerns

1. Establish a task force composed of academic vice-presidents, deans, and department chairpersons to examine current academic programs. This task force should

a. Analyze the attitudes of faculty and staff toward institutional admission of diverse student groups

b. Develop program initiatives that flow from institutional taskforce findings and outline departmental goals for specific nontraditional disciplines.

2. Commit resources, based on the results of departmental assessments, to increase the number of minority and women students in nontraditional academic programs.

Program Concerns

The program should reinforce comprehensive institutional goals for minorities and women.

1. Create an environment designed to enhance the intellectual development of minorities and women by exposing them to representative role models. This environment should include
   a. An awareness of ethnic and racial attitudes
   b. A reexamination of the curricula to reduce gender and racial bias
   c. The development of seminars, workshops, and guest lecture series that invite minorities and women as keynote speakers.
2. Develop relationships with elementary and secondary schools to identify and cultivate potential students for nontraditional careers.
3. Implement precollege programs that provide academic assistance for underprepared students.
4. Determine institutional barriers to the advancement of minorities and women in such nontraditional areas as science, computer science, and engineering. (For example, determine the number of minorities and women on the faculty and the number of minority and women students, then develop strategies to create support systems within departments.)

Faculty Role

1. Involve faculty in activities that promote the social, psychological, and educational development of minorities and women students.
2. Establish mentor relationships with minority and women students.
3. Hire more minorities and women as faculty in nontraditional disciplines. If full-time faculty are unavailable, explore alternative arrangements such as
   a. Offering part-time appointments
   b. Utilizing loaned executives from corporations.

Student Support Services

1. Establish a series of in-service training sessions to enhance the skills of faculty and staff who work with minorities and women by developing cross-cultural counseling strategies and delivery of services to these students.
2. Develop collaborative relationships with existing special programs that serve minorities and women.
3. Develop collaborative relationships with faculty to explore concerns expressed by minorities and women, especially how they are treated in nontraditional disciplines.
4. Encourage the development of new learning options for older women by
   a. Providing for independent study opportunities
   b. Providing credit for work experiences.
5. Make services available to women by
   a. Assisting in providing child-care opportunities
   b. Establishing seminars for women to discuss their work
   c. Providing flexible scheduling to accommodate learning options for women.
6. Make financial aid funds available to students. (This is crucial to the retention of minority students.)
7. Develop workshops that focus on the development of those pursuing nontraditional careers. These workshops should include experiences that facilitate
   a. Learning to take control of one's educational experiences by learning to be assertive without being aggressive
   b. Utilizing faculty and professional staff to assist in understanding the three primary career exploration categories: self-exploration, exploration of the world of work, and career decision making
   c. Maximizing relationships with key people, including faculty staff, and peers
   d. Establishing goals for careers and professions by identifying the kinds of educational experiences that will enhance one's course of study
   e. Identifying career options that are both vertical (for upward mobility) and horizontal (for lateral mobility) in career decision making
   f. Establishing goals for career and profession by identifying the educational experiences that will enhance one's course of study.
8. Develop a data base that documents student experiences, performance level, and feedback as an outgrowth of the support services provided.

Conclusion

If the enrollment and retention of minorities and women is a serious institutional goal, then intervention strategies must be implemented to increase the number of minorities and women. If educational institutions continue to ignore issues related to minorities and women, they discard a potentially valuable pool of human energy and creativity.

References

Anderson, O., and others. "Achieving Sex Equity for Minority Women." In S. Klein (ed.), *Handbook for Achieving Sex Equity Through Education.* Baltimore: Johns Hopkins Press, 1984.

Astin, A. W. *Minorities in American Higher Education.* San Francisco: Jossey-Bass, 1982.

Axelson, L. "Socialization and Career Orientation Among Black and White College Women." *Journal of Vocational Behavior,* 1974, 5, 307–319.

Dunteman, G. H., and others. *Race and Sex Differences in College Science Program Participation.* Triangle Park, N.C.: Research Triangle Institute, 1979.

Epstein, C. F. "Positive Effect of the Multiple Negative: Explaining the Success of Black Professional Women." *American Journal of Sociology,* 1973, 78, 912–935.

Hodgkinson, H. L. "Demographics of Education, Kindergarten Through Graduate School." Washington, D.C.: Institute for Educational Leadership, 1985.

Holliday, G. "Addressing the Concerns of Returning Students." In N. Evans (ed.), *Facilitating the Development of Women.* New Directions for Student Services, no. 29. San Francisco: Jossey-Bass, 1985.

Jackson, J. "Black Women in a Racist Society." In C. Willie (ed.), *Racism in Mental Health.* Pittsburgh, Pa.: University of Pittsburgh Press, 1974.

Kanter, R. M. "Some Effects of Proportion on Groups Life: Skewed Ratios and Responses to Token Women." *American Journal of Sociology,* 1975, 82, 965–990.

Kingdon, M. A., and Sedlacek, W. "Differences Between Who Chooses Traditional and Nontraditional Careers." *Journal of the National Association of Women Deans, Administrators, and Counselors,* 1982, 42 (2), 34–36.

Knudson, M. A. "Young Management Women: A New Look." *Journal of the National Association of Women Deans, Administrators, and Counselors,* 1982, 45 (2), 3–9.

Pappas, J. P., and Loring, R. K. "Returning Learners." In L. Noel, R. Levitz, D. Saluri, and Associates (eds.), *Increasing Student Retention.* San Francisco: Jossey-Bass, 1985.

Sandler, B., and Hall, R. "The Classroom Climate, A Chilly One for Women." Washington, D.C.: Project on the Status of Women, Association of American Colleges, 1982.

Scott, P. B. "Preparing Black Women for Non-Traditional Professions: Some Considerations for Career Counseling." *Journal of the National Association of Women Deans, Administrators, and Counselors,* 1977, 40 (4), 135–139.

Scott, P. B., and Hohrn, M. "A Pilot Study of Black Female Undergraduates as Majors in Non-traditional Curricula at University of Knoxville." Unpublished report, University of Knoxville, 1975.

Terborg, J. R. "Women in Management: A Research Review." *Journal of Applied Psychology,* 1977, 62, 647–664.

Trent, W. "Equality Considerations in Higher Education: Race and Sex Differences in Degree Attainment and Major Field from 1976 through 1981." *American Journal of Education,* May 1984, p. 302.

Carol J. Carter is associate director of the African–American Institute and Assistant Dean at Northeastern University in Boston, Massachusetts. She has served as assistant director of the Higher Education Resource Services (HERS) at Bryn Mawr College in Bryn Mawr, Pennsylvania.

*Before committing itself to new career programs, a higher
education institution should answer some basic questions
about the program's implications for faculty development.*

Professors and Professional
Programs: Fostering Mutually
Beneficial Development

Roger G. Baldwin

Degree programs with titles remarkably similar to occupational categories
in the employment section of a newspaper are proliferating at colleges
and universities across the United States. Even prestigious institutions
that pride themselves on their commitment to the liberal arts are adding
majors or minors in professional fields in response to the demands of
career-oriented students.

    Altering the curriculum of a higher education institution affects all
components of an academic organization, especially faculty members.
Before adding new programs in business, computer science, or other areas
with obvious career applications, any responsible college or university
would carefully project the implications of such action. Standard questions
about potential program expenses, enrollment trends, space utilization,
and equipment costs are fundamental to deliberations concerning the feasibility of proposed academic programs. Other chapters in this sourcebook
address mission, budgetary, legal, and accreditation issues that should be
debated prior to the establishment of new career programs. In a period
of restricted resources, no college president wants to commit funds care-
lessly—even to highly popular professional education areas.

M.A.F. Rehnke (ed.). *Creating Career Programs in a Liberal Arts Context.*
New Directions for Higher Education, no. 57. San Francisco: Jossey-Bass, Spring 1987.

The implications of adding career programs for the professional development of new and continuing faculty members deserve equally serious consideration. The overall health and vitality of a college or university is closely related to the ability of its faculty to respond to shifting enrollment patterns and an evolving educational mission. Yet, it is a rare higher education institution that thoroughly considers how the addition of one or more programs can alter the work environment and professional development needs of its instructional staff. Before committing itself to new program initiatives, a higher education institution should also ponder some basic questions concerning staffing practices and professional development needs. Faculty committees, department chairpersons, academic administrators, and individual professors should each address questions such as

- What types of professional expertise and skills will be needed to implement the proposed program?
- Which of these are already available among current faculty?
- Is it feasible to retrain current professors to teach in the new career program rather than hire additional personnel?
- Could a cooperative, interdisciplinary career program be developed rather than adding an entirely new, separate, and costly enclave that may compete with established academic programs?
- What forms of support for faculty development can facilitate the establishment of a successful career program while enhancing overall instititutional morale?

Informed and thoughtful answers to each of these questions should better prepare a college to assess realistically the merits of adding one or more career programs to its curriculum. They should also help the institution to utilize fully its faculty resources in support of any new programs it decides to initiate.

Keep Faculty Informed and Encourage Their Involvement

The success of new academic ventures depends on the cooperation and support of faculty members, both those who are indirectly as well as directly affected. Hence, a fundamental principle is to keep the faculty in general informed and, where possible, involved in the development of new career programs. Methods of achieving this objective, of course, will vary according to the nature of the institution. Reports in campus newsletters, discussions in department meetings, special presentations, and open forums to consider proposed programs can be employed. Such dialogue could lead to cooperation among established faculty members and professors associated with new professional programs. Invigorating conversations of intellectual issues, impromptu sessions on teaching practices, and jointly authored new course proposals are among the valuable outcomes that may result. Ideally, efforts to involve professors in the planning of new academic initiatives will enhance faculty commitment to program success. Perhaps more important, they may help professors identify exciting new outlets for their own career development.

Development Implications for Faculty in General

Information on Career-Oriented Students. New academic programs typically attract different types of students with distinct interests, abilities, and educational needs. These students take courses throughout the institution and hence present new challenges to a broad spectrum of professors. Special professional development services can help prepare faculty to work effectively with students enrolled in new career programs. The best ways to assist faculty again depend on the character and traditions of an institution. Weekend workshops with external consultants, presentations at faculty meetings, and brown-bag lunches are some of the techniques that can be employed effectively. The format of faculty development activities can vary almost as much as the content.

Professors should have an opportunity to learn about the common attributes of students enrolled in career programs. Information on the aptitudes, abilities, and especially the preferred learning styles of career-oriented students should help college teachers tailor their course objectives, assignments, and class activities to foster learning in an efficient manner. Information on the interests and goals of such students, likewise, can help professors design courses that support students' educational objectives. (For further information on career-oriented students, see Chapter Ten, this volume.)

Strategies for Teaching and Advising. Today, all undergraduates, not just those in professional education programs, seem worried about the relationship between their educational experiences and the employment sector they hope to enter on graduation. Relating formal education to these vocational concerns can be very challenging to college professors. The difficult task for the teacher is to incorporate career issues and information into courses that previously have lacked a conscious connection with the work world. How can they clearly demonstrate the employment-related knowledge, values, and skills developed in traditional academic disciplines?

Some teaching-learning strategies common in professional education programs can help professors tie their courses to the postcollege world of employment. Professional fields such as business, engineering, and social work have for years experimented with ways to relate theoretical and scientific knowledge in their fields to actual practice. Professors in all academic areas can benefit from learning how to employ many of these techniques in their classes.

Problem-focused interdisciplinary courses are a practical educational tool developed to a high degree by some professional fields. Professors in the traditional disciplines have much to learn about problem-centered teaching from their colleagues in business, law, and social work, for instance. These professional fields offer courses such as portfolio management and family law that focus on specific issues and tasks their students are likely to encounter following graduation.

Some instructional methods frequently employed in professional education classes can help professors demonstrate vocational applications of more traditional disciplines and concurrently enhance the learning that occurs in career-based programs. Case studies and simulations present theoretical concepts or principles in practical problem situations. Role playing, likewise, encourages students to apply their course work directly to challenging circumstances. Inviting active practitioners to speak in classes is another professional education strategy faculty in general should have in their repertoire of instructional methods. Practitioners can help forge a direct link between the classroom and the corporation or government agency by identifying the knowledge and skills these institutions employ on the job and by discussing the type of educational background necessary for success in their field. These guests can also enhance student performance by serving as positive role models.

Experiential learning opportunities (such as internships, practicums, and field trips) represent another method educators in professional fields can employ to link theory and practice. Professors unfamiliar with this nontraditional educational strategy should learn about its merits as a device for connecting formal education with various employment sectors. Likewise, they should become familiar with the critical role an instructor plays in planning, supervising, and evaluating experiential learning.

General student advising is another faculty activity that may be altered by the addition of career-focused academic programs. Traditionally, academic advising has centered predominantly on questions concerning the student's major and graduation requirements. In contrast, advising in professional fields has given more attention to career concerns and job placement. Before they feel competent to expand their duties as advisers, professors in many disciplines may desire an advising workshop or other opportunity to enhance their preparation to counsel students effectively.

The addition of career programs presents challenges for faculty in all parts of a higher education institution. Fortunately, development of new courses and novel teaching strategies can provide a refreshing expansion of professors' careers at the same time such activities respond to students' desire for challenging learning experiences that relate directly to their vocational goals.

Grants to Promote Professional Development. Structured workshops, seminars, and discussion groups can satisfy only a portion of the professional development needs stimulated by new career programs. Activities planned by administrators and faculty committees should therefore be supplemented by learning projects designed by individual professors or two or three collaborating colleagues. Competitive small grant programs are ideally suited to stimulate this type of effort. Professors could request grants from their institution to develop expertise in an area related to a new career program. Two mathematics professors, for example, might request support to develop a computer science course for newly arrived business students. Ideally, such a grant program would result in more efficient use of existing faculty resources and encourage cooperation among professors in arts and sciences and professional areas. Students, of course, will be direct beneficiaries of faculty growth and vitality engendered by a small grant program.

Locating funds to support professional development through small grants is always a challenge. When adding a career program, one useful tactic would be for a college or university to approach the regional and national employers and professional associations that would eventually benefit from the new program. These groups might be willing to pay for the design of relevant course materials or to cover the salary of the temporary replacement for a faculty member receiving course development funds. Another strategy, of course, is to encourage professors to seek outside funds for development activities relevant to new career programs. For example, an academic dean or department chair could give a professor a one-course reduced load or subsidize travel to a specialized library or a clinical setting to enable him or her to prepare a proposal for funding by a private foundation or government agency.

Retraining and Retooling Professors

Recruiting faculty for new career programs is a costly process and can encumber an institution with long-term personnel commitments. A feasible alternative in some cases is to retrain professors to teach primarily in new programs. Given the interdisciplinary nature of most professional fields, it is likely that there are some current professors in the natural sciences, and the humanities who, with a modest amount of additional preparation, could be employed productively in career programs. Several options are available to accomplish this objective. One is to set up a temporary retraining program intended to move current professors into certain new or growing fields. Some large institutions, such as California State University at Long Beach, have employed this technique to accomplish quite specific retraining goals (Baldwin and others, 1981). A second alternative is for a college or university to develop a retraining policy aimed at individual faculty members who wish to prepare to transfer into another instructional field. Moderate-sized institutions where only small numbers of professors are likely to wish to retrain have tended to employ this more individualized approach. Schools such as Mary College in North Dakota and the College of Saint Scholastica in Minnesota have implemented quite innovative retraining policies (Rice, 1985). A third strategy is particularly appropriate for preparing faculty members to work in career programs. Professors at some colleges and universities may participate in an internship or practicum in a corporation, government agency, or other organization to acquire knowledge and skills applicable to academic programs on their home campus. Birmingham-Southern College in Alabama and Furman University in South Carolina are among the institutions that have experimented with faculty internships and practicums (Baldwin and others, 1981). Practical experience of this nature can help college teachers transfer their theoretical expertise to more applied professional fields.

Support for Part-Time and Temporary Faculty

Too often faculty development policies and programs fail to include adjunct faculty members. This unfortunate oversight should be corrected when a college or university adds career-oriented programs. Traditionally, business, journalism, and other professional areas have welcomed active practitioners to their instructional staffs on a part-time or temporary basis. These individuals bring technical expertise and a front-line perspective to an academic program, but they also bring special needs that an educational institution should recognize. Most adjunct instructors have limited knowledge of the college or university that employs them. They are unfamiliar with its academic policies, standards, and the services it provides. Similarly, they know little about the nature of its students. Perhaps more important, professional practitioners may lack experience as teachers.

Certainly institutions that wish to derive the maximum benefit from adjunct professors in career programs should offer appropriate forms of faculty development assistance. Some effort to orient adjunct faculty to the institution and to their teaching responsibilities is desirable. Some effort to help new teachers prepare syllabi and course assignments and to plan class activities, even if this simply consists of occasional conversations with the department chair, should be very beneficial. Temporary and part-time teachers should also receive institutional directories and policy manuals that can help them deal with unanticipated problems and questions. Likewise, they should be included on faculty mailing lists and other campus information networks that keep members of the academic community apprised of important issues. Adjunct faculty who maintain a long-term commitment to a career program in an academic institution deserve support for their professional development as well. They should be welcome to participate in faculty workshops and seminars. Also, they should be eligible to apply for research grants and funds to attend professional conferences. Obviously, full-time faculty must be an institution's highest priority when support for professional development is distributed. But it would be a waste of valuable human talent not to foster the professional vitality of adjunct instructors too.

Career Change and Outplacement

The addition of career-oriented academic programs may require some difficult personnel decisions. Faculty positions in declining or underenrolled areas may have to be terminated to make funds available for new positions. In some cases, positions can be reallocated through natural attrition. In others, underutilized professors can be moved into new programs as they are established or into administrative posts. A happy marriage between some professors and their restructured institution, however, cannot always be achieved. In such cases, assistance with career change to another higher education institution or a different professional endeavor may be advisable. Assistance to displaced professors can ease their transition to a new career challenge. Perhaps just as important, it can help to protect the morale of remaining faculty members by demonstrating that they work for a humane and supportive college or university.

Outplacement must be a very individualized process. Nevertheless, there are several things an institution can do to assist professors whose departure has been provoked by a redistribution of institutional resources. Certainly the services of the career planning and placement office should be available to professors seeking to make a career change. This should include individual counseling on a confidential basis if desired. In addition, upper-level administrators, appropriate department chairs, and, in some cases, board of trustee members should employ their various professional networks to help professors locate suitable new positions. If the institution's ability to assist in career change is limited, it may be appropriate to hire a private outplacement service to aid faculty members with the career transition process. (For further discussion, see Chapter Five, this volume.)

Conclusions and Recommendations

The decision to add new career-oriented programs to the curriculum of a college or university requires careful assessment of many important issues, not the least of which is the institution's fundamental educational mission. Under these circumstances it is easy to overlook less immediate concerns such as the faculty development implications of adding programs of this sort. However, over the long term the way a college or university helps its faculty adapt to revisions in its educational program can be just as significant to its vigor and effectiveness as a higher education institution.

The lack of understanding, almost enmity, that once characterized relations between traditional academic disciplines and applied fields has diminished. Educators in professional areas and those in arts and sciences now readily acknowledge that they have a lot to learn from each other as well as a lot to contribute. The addition of career-oriented programs to the curriculum of a college or university, if done properly, should do more than increase enrollment figures; it should enhance institutional vitality by adding a wide range of stimulating educational challenges and opportunities for professors' career development.

These positive by-products may not be immediately obvious to faculty members or administrators. Considerable thought and discussion throughout an academic community will be necessary to identify the range of professional development implications likely to accompany new career-related programs. Careful responses to the five questions presented at the beginning of this chapter should help an institution take full advantage of the potential posed by novel program initiatives.

References

Baldwin, R., Brakeman, L., Edgerton, R., Hagberg, J. and Maher, T. *Expanding Faculty Options: Career Development Projects at Colleges and Universities.* Washington, D.C.: American Association for Higher Education, 1981.

Rice, R. E. *Faculty Lives: Vitality and Change.* Saint Paul, Minn.: Northwest Area Foundation, 1985.

Roger G. Baldwin is assistant professor of higher education at the College of William and Mary in Williamsburg, Virginia. His research focuses on the academic workplace and the career development of college professors. He is editor of Incentives for Faculty Vitality, *a* New Directions for Higher Education *sourcebook (1985).*

Integration of career and liberal study programs can be educationally fruitful if similarities and differences in influences and ideologies are recognized. At an early stage, discussions should focus on compatible learning activities and outcomes.

Liberal Education and Professional Programs: Conflict, Coexistence, or Compatibility?

Joan S. Stark

Over the last 150 years debates about the purpose of American higher education frequently have posed education for life and education for a career as conflicting goals. Although the debate continues, for pragmatic reasons the two types of education now coexist in most universities and in some liberal arts colleges. Although in large public colleges student demand has allowed conflict to be replaced by coexistence, small institutions with limited resources must carefully assess priorities and student educational purposes to achieve compatibility of liberal and vocational education. Few students still desire to pursue postsecondary education in separate phases; most enter college with multiple purposes that include both liberal education and career objectives. These goals are not mutually exclusive or inconsistent but can be blended in ways beneficial to students, society, and institutional survival.

The author appreciates partial support of this work by the Fund for the Improvement of Postsecondary Education.

M.A.F. Rehnke (ed.). *Creating Career Programs in a Liberal Arts Context.*
New Directions for Higher Education, no. 57. San Francisco: Jossey-Bass, Spring 1987.

In planning to introduce or expand career programs, liberal arts colleges need to be aware of unique characteristics of professional programs. It is important to recognize that such programs involve (1) special relationships with the external environment, (2) faculty with varying backgrounds and orientations, (3) specific intended educational outcomes, (4) a broad range of curricular debates, and (5) specific types of educational activities. In discussing the first two of these dimensions, this chapter will emphasize characteristics that may differentiate professional programs from liberal arts programs. In discussing the last three dimensions, avenues of potential compatibility and integration of career and liberal arts missions will be stressed.

Although detailed discussion of data and methodology are inappropriate here, the generalizations in this chapter are based on a synthesis of recent literature in twelve fields of professional education (Stark, Lowther, and Hagerty, 1986c), drawn from a 1985 survey responses of 2,230 educators in 10 professional fields at 346 colleges and universities (Stark, Lowther, and Hagerty, 1986a, 1986b), and generally follow a conceptual framework for studying preservice professional study in four-year institutions (Stark, Lowther, Hagerty, and Orczyk, 1986).

Relationships with the External Environment

Societal views and trends may have more direct effects on professional programs than on liberal arts programs. In addition to the general economy, societal rewards for professionals (both status and compensation), available job opportunities, images of the professional field conveyed by the media, and support from both private and government sources are particularly potent influences. Variations in societal support for professional programs may affect students and programs directly as well as indirectly. Although trends in societal support vary, our data indicate that faculty members in service-oriented professions such as education, nursing, social work, and library science feel that society is not supportive of their fields, while faculty members in more enterprising fields such as engineering and business feel that society values their work. Faculty in journalism and architecture feel there is modest societal support for their professions. Such assessments of societal esteem may influence faculty activities and contributions to the college mission.

In addition to the influence of society, each professional program relates to a community of professional practitioners who desire and may insist on a participatory voice in program planning. In all fields faculty perceive the strongest professional influence to come from the specialized accrediting agencies. Since program accreditation is more important to graduates in professional fields than regional accreditation is to liberal arts graduates, specialized accrediting agencies may be somewhat more prescriptive about curriculum, facilities, and faculty qualifications than are the more inclusive regional accrediting associations. (For further discussion of this issue, see Chapter Six, this volume.) Influence is also exerted by professional publications, availability of practice settings, and practitioner groups. Nursing, social work, and engineering faculty report the highest levels of influence from their professional communities. Professional community influences in architecture, education, journalism, and library science seem to be more modest. In keeping with professional community norms, however, it may be important for the liberal arts college to offer students in these and other fields degree designations other than the traditional bachelor of arts degree. In no professional fields do faculty currently perceive any significant attempt to control the number of new graduates.

Faculty Background and Orientation

The backgrounds of professional program faculty often differ from those of liberal arts faculty and from each other. For example, qualified candidates for faculty positions in architecture, business, journalism, and nursing may hold a professional master's degree rather than a doctorate as their highest degree. Additionally, education, journalism, and nursing faculty members typically will have spent several years as professional practitioners before entering academe; this is less likely to be true of engineering faculty members. Still, architecture and engineering faculty may wish to avail themselves of plentiful opportunities to continue their professional practice on a part-time basis. Because of these differences, addition of professional faculty to a liberal arts college may require some new understandings concerning salaries, promotional opportunities, and the balance of obligations on and off campus.

Professional-field faculty who enter the liberal arts setting are likely to endorse, or come to endorse, its general undergraduate mission as they link their role as teachers with their former or continuing roles as practitioners and expert consultants. Although it is impossible to know whether the setting influences the preferred role or vice versa, it appears that professional-field faculty currently employed in teaching institutions more frequently endorse combined roles of teaching and professional practice, while those in the same fields employed in research institutions (and more likely to hold doctorates) strongly combine a research orientation with their teaching roles (Stark, Lowther, and Hagerty, 1986b).

However, professional-field faculty may have little experience in teaching students with undeveloped career goals or those from other professional fields. There may be more need in a liberal arts college than in a large university for professional-field faculty to also contribute to the liberal arts program. Some deliberate effort may be necessary to introduce them to a variety of teaching roles.

Outcomes of Professional Preparation

Although there are variations among fields, professional-field faculty members strongly endorse at least eleven specific outcomes for their graduates. It is useful to examine these outcomes in relation to goals of liberal education (Stark, 1986) (see Figure 1). For ease of discussion, outcomes specific to professional education will be referred to as traditional professional competences (TPCs), and the set potentially coincident with liberal arts objectives will be referred to as liberal education objectives (LEOs).

TPC outcomes include the concepts and principles to be learned (many of which may draw on the basic liberal arts disciplines), the technical skills to be mastered, and the integration of this theoretical and practical knowledge, usually in an applicable field setting.

Although we have labeled TPC outcomes as traditionally professional, the case can be made that these dimensions have analogs in liberal study as outcomes of the major or specialization. In-depth study of a discipline requires such elements as (1) a critical core of method and theory, (2) a variety of analytic tools for problem solving, (3) a sequence that presumes advancing sophistication, and (4) demonstration of mastery. Some would add career exploration as an outcome of liberal study, considering career marketability in a professional field as a more advanced stage of student development.

As might be expected, professional-field faculty strongly endorse conceptual and integrative competence as essential for their graduates. Unexpectedly, however, faculty members in fields such as business, engineering, and architecture endorse technical competence much less strongly. These attitudes may reflect a reaction to recent criticism of professional study as excessively narrow and specialized or may result from beliefs in these particular fields that technical skills are best learned on the specific job. In contrast, faculty members in nursing, social work, education, and library science, who more typically organize and closely supervise field experiences as part of undergraduate education, believe that technical competence deserves considerable emphasis. Faculty views of the importance of career marketability also contradict prevailing occupational stereotypes. Although professional faculty are certainly likely to place different demands on the career placement service than the liberal arts faculty, they are unlikely to see job placement as their highest program priority.

Although professional field faculty place the highest emphasis on TPC outcomes, they are only slightly less likely to endorse liberal education (LEO) outcomes. The two types of outcomes are not at all distinct (in our survey their correlation is more than 0.50) and as curricular plans are devised, they may be inseparable. To advance the notion of compatibility of liberal and career education, we will discuss each of the LEO outcomes.

Figure 1. Professional Education Outcomes

Outcome	Definition
Traditional Professional Competences	
Conceptual Competence	The graduate should understand the body of knowledge that is basic to practice of the profession; that is, the theoretical base or the professional knowledge base.
Technical Competence	The graduate should be able to perform the fundamental skills or tasks required in professional practice.
Integrative Competence	The graduate should be able to integrate theory and practice; that is, select the knowledge and skills applicable to a particular professional work setting or problem.
Career Marketability	The graduate should not only meet basic standards for entrance into the profession (such as licensing or certification where they exist) but also be a competitive applicant for a beginning position.
Short-Term Liberal Education Outcomes	
Communication Competence	The graduate should be able to use written and oral communication effectively.
Contextual Competence	The graduate should understand the social, environmental, economic, and cultural setting in which the profession is practiced.
Professional Identity	The graduate should have developed an identification with the professional role.
Professional Ethics	The graduate should know and apply ethical principles and professional conduct standards of the professional field.
Long-Range Liberal Education Outcomes	
Adaptive Competence	The graduate should demonstrate the ability to anticipate and adapt to changes in society and technology that are important to the profession.
Scholarly Concern for Improvement of the Profession	The graduate should be willing to cooperate with or participate in research or other scholarly activities that improve professional practice.
Motivation for Continued Learning	The graduate should actively seek opportunities to update professional knowledge.

Communication Competence. The connection between communication competence of professional students and the goals of liberal education needs little exposition. Few would disagree that reading, writing, and speaking are necessary skills both to professional practice and to informed citizenry. Additionally, in our society these skills are necessary vehicles for personal and professional growth. Professional educators feel, as do liberal arts educators, that communication skills deserve strong emphasis.

Contextual Competence. If an educated person should have an enlarged understanding of reality and make judgments based on an understanding of historical, social, economic, scientific, and political realities, certainly no less is demanded of the same individual acting in a professional role. The capability to adopt multiple perspectives also allows the graduate to comprehend the complex interdependencies between the profession and society.

Although professionals would differ concerning what aspects of the environment are most relevant to professional practice, they are generally in agreement that contextual competence is important. Unfortunately, in many universities there is a trend for professional educators to teach contextual courses within their own programs in order to ensure content relevance rather than relying on liberal arts requirements or electives to provide necessary context.

Professional Identity. It is easy to grasp abstractly the relationship of our concept of professional identity to liberal learning goals and difficult to make the connection concrete.

For many in our complex, mobile, and frequently impersonal society, the work setting has replaced more traditional personal anchors— church, family, and local community. Thus professional identity both parallels and supplements the liberal education goal of developing a feeling of personal identity. The Association of American Colleges (AAC) report (1985, p. 16) indicates that a baccalaureate education "should lead young men and women to a satisfying possession of themselves." It advocates practice in writing as a vehicle for achieving personal identity. Similarly, educational philospher Thomas Green asserts that a sense of personal worth and self-confidence can also develop from the experience of "being good at doing something," hence, the use of the phrase "to practice" a discipline or profession (Green, 1981). Professional practice, which often includes a satisfying or altruistic client relationship, may be a second effective vehicle for developing possession of one's self and gaining a sense of one's place in the world as an individual and citizen.

Although all respondents in our survey considered professional identity quite important, faculty in different professional fields place different emphases on this outcome. Faculty in nursing, social work, education, journalism, and library science appear more likely to be concerned with professional socialization experiences specifically intended to develop identity with the professional role. Possibly because of an already crowded curriculum, faculty members in business and engineering typically depend on unstructured experiences to nurture this attitude, and some view professional identity as currently overemphasized in their programs.

Professional Ethics. Nearly all discussions of the goals of liberal learning include development of ethical standards as a major goal. When courses are specifically developed to achieve this goal, instructors often construct ethical dilemmas in the form of case studies for student consideration. In every professional field new entrants face choices and responsibilities; the AAC report (1985, p. 27) calls this "the difficult enterprise of making interpretive decisions and facing up to their full consequences." Ethical studies represent a natural, realistic, and relevant link between liberal and professional education. All professional-field faculty recognize ethics as an important outcome, but there is disagreement about the means of implementation.

Adaptive Competence. A liberally educated person has an enhanced capacity to anticipate and adapt to social changes that are occurring at an exponential rate. Since professional practice is dynamic rather than static, professionals must sense and detect needed changes in practice and take steps to initiate new procedures.

Typically, the curriculum in most professional preparation programs is under constant examination and responsive to changing needs and expectations of society. Futurists tell us, however, that humans have limited capacity to conceptualize the future, and this may be reflected in our finding that faculty in most professional fields view development of adaptive competence among entry-level professional students as deserving of slightly less emphasis than some of the other outcomes.

Scholarly Concern for Improvement. Every discussion of liberal education specifies thinking skills as the heart of the intellectual process, with emphasis on a spirit of inquiry, critical analysis, scientific inquiry, observation and inference, and logical thinking. Recent discussions have revived the idea that these habits of mind developed through liberal study are transferable to other settings such as work.

In professional study similar skills are developed as theory and practice are integrated. But what of the longer-range goal of applying that spirit of inquiry to the future, specifically to the future of the profession? One demonstration that liberal goals have been met would be evidence that explicit attention is given in entry-level professional preparation to creating new ways to examine and improve professional practice. Such attention might engender among students a sense of obligation to participate in research and development. Unexpectedly, professional-field faculty members rate developing a scholarly concern for improvement among entry-level students as low in importance compared to other professional outcomes.

Motivation for Continued Learning. Closely linked to a spirit of scholarly concern is attention to personal and professional development. An educated person will understand the need to continue learning throughout life. Professional faculty, like liberal arts faculty, believe that substantial emphasis should be placed on fostering a sense of motivation for continued learning. Attitudes vary on how much motivation should be fostered at the entry-level and may reflect differences among professional fields concerning the locus of responsibility for initiating and funding continuing education of the professional employee.

Nature of Curricular Debates

Despite the possibility of responsiveness to societal trends and issues, there is little evidence that professional-program faculty engage in curriculum debate more extensively than do faculty in general. In fact, some recent investigations provide evidence that there is little debate about curricular issues in fields such as engineering, where strong agreement exists on what concepts and modes of inquiry are to be taught (Creswell and Roskens, 1981). This research suggests that debate is likely to be more extensive in fields such as education and social work, where a variety of conceptual perspectives, methodologies, and applications are entertained.

Nonetheless, there are some distinct issues that may characterize programmatic discussion among professional field faculty. Just as liberal arts faculties may debate whether they should be attending to students' career development, professional-field faculty debate the appropriate balance of theory and practice in the curriculum, the nature and assessment of the practice or clinical experience, and the relation to and integration of foundation courses in other fields. Currently, relations with liberal arts courses are discussed most actively in education (probably based on recent public criticism of new graduates) but less actively in journalism, where accrediting standards mandate a majority of liberal arts courses.

Program length is an issue in several fields. Engineering faculty find it difficult to compress what they believe to be essential content into a four-year period; in education there is considerable discussion about extending programs to five years. Related to program length are discussions about obligations to provide continuing education for professionals. Depending on other locally available opportunities, a liberal arts college that adopts programs where the individual practitioner rather than the employer is responsible for continuing professional development may soon find pressures building to move toward credit or noncredit graduate programs. Additionally, although few professional programs except education are currently debating admissions criteria or the number of students who should graduate in each field, increasingly popular programs such as business require that additional resources be devoted to their efforts in the interests of equity. Such demands based on shifting student interests may heighten rather than resolve tensions regarding resource allocation in the liberal arts college.

Types of Educational Activities

The most characteristic part of a professional preparation program is the practicum, internship, or clinical experience where the student is guided in integrating theoretical knowledge and technical skills. For most fields, providing opportunities for practicum experiences requires that relationships with the practice field be established and maintained. For a variety of reasons (including such factors as unionization of professional practitioners, state laws concerning licensing standards, liability and workmen's compensation insurance), such relationships may be expensive and politically difficult to maintain. If a liberal arts college is located in a nonurban area, it may be necessary to provide organized arrangements for student transportation or housing. Often student participation in extracurricular activities and other types of campus involvement must be sacrificed in these instances.

Professional programs depend fairly heavily on a variety of special types of extracurricular activities for socialization of graduates into the professional field. Such activities, which may require new budget appropriations, include field trips, guest speakers, and student attendance at conferences.

However, there are a variety of educational activities professional students may pursue that can serve several professional programs and provide additional breadth for liberal arts students. Incorporation of some career programs in a liberal arts curriculum provides established channels through which undecided students may pursue guided career exploration on a more limited basis than offered by a lengthy internship. Speakers and conferences brought to the campus by the career programs can provide new opportunities and a sense of relevance to students whose experience with the resolution of pressing social issues has been limited to classroom discussion.

A variety of potentially efficient and educationally attractive examples of collaboration between professional and liberal arts programs exist including the examples that follow.

Cooperative courses in ethics may incorporate dilemmas faced by both citizens and professionals and may help foster a sense of realism and commitment. It seems important that nursing faculty foster both ethical standards and professional identity in courses called nursing leadership; this model could be used by other fields.

Communication skills for graduates in nearly all professional fields extend beyond reading and writing skills to include listening, interviewing, public speaking, client empathy, and group relations skills. Such aspects of communication, if they can be incorporated into the English or social science curricula, may provide needed breadth for all students.

Meeting the needs of a diverse national and international population is a concern of fields such as nursing, education, social work, and library science. Such efforts are consistent with liberal education goals of reducing student provincialism.

Courses in research methods can foster critical thinking skills and are particularly likely to do so if they deal with the real problems that face students preparing for professional practice. The generic methods of problem solving used in engineering, for example, are already recognized as applicable to more general thinking strategies.

Finally, as technology changes our society, both liberal arts students and students in career programs will need to be aware of technology's utility and potential to change society in basic ways. Consideration of technological change from the standpoint of professional practice as well as from the point of view of an educated citizen may provide a balanced perspective.

Developing Compatibility

Liberal arts colleges that consider adding career programs are often involved in intense debates about the possible advantages and disadvantages to the institution, its students, and its faculty. Too frequently such debates are based on limited information about professional programs, and they focus on practical or financial matters rather than on educational outcomes. Although the details will depend on which new programs are being discussed, the following list summarizes some pragmatic issues that should be attended to in early planning stages.

1. The college must analyze and deal in advance with potential problems of
   a. Expense incurred in field experiences
   b. Political and financial implications of external influences and relationships
   c. Differentiation of faculty obligations, salaries, and promotions standards
   d. Diversity of scholarly effort
   e. Unique counseling, transportation, and residence needs of career-directed students.
2. Each faculty sector must be prepared to recognize, understand, and respect the basis of the other's differing conception of educational purpose and process. For example, liberal arts faculty must be aware of the need of professional faculty to spend time in the field rather than in the library or laboratory. Professional

faculty must be aware that liberal arts faculty do not as frequently espouse a utilitarian purpose for education and may view student credentials for admission differently.

3. The college must recognize that introducing programs with varied educational orientations may invite further pressures for programmatic expansion such as continuing education or professional graduate work and for reallocation of resources previously devoted to liberal learning.

Summary

Although such considerations are important, too often discussions of the major issues of curriculum and student learning are delayed until decisions have been made, faculty hired or retrained, and professional programs begun. When initiated at an early juncture, fruitful discussion and ideas for educationally productive collaboration can convert discussions from an opportunistic focus to one that focuses on creation of opportunities. A college considering new professional programs might well invite to campus professional faculty from other institutions for an intensive examination of the list of congruent liberal and professional education outcomes we have provided. The discussion could also hypothetically extend to the kinds of collaborative learning activities that will achieve these outcomes and benefit both liberal arts and career students. Focusing discussion on objectives and activities that serve the needs of both sectors concurrently is likely to lead to compatibility rather than uneasy coexistence.

References

Association of American Colleges. *Report of the Project on Redefining the Meaning and Purpose of Baccalaureate Degrees: Integrity in the College Curriculum.* Washington, D.C.: Association of American Colleges, 1985.

Creswell, J. W., and Roskens, R. W. "The Biglan Studies of Differences Among Academic Areas." *Review of Higher Education*, 1981, *4* (3), 1-16.

Green, T. "On Competence." In A. W. Chickering and Associates (ed.), *The Modern American College.* San Francisco: Jossey-Bass, 1981.

Stark, J. S. "Liberal Outcomes of Professional Preparation." Division I invited address presented at the American Educational Research Association, San Francisco, April 16-20, 1986.

Stark, J. S., Lowther, M. A., and Hagerty, B.M.K. "Faculty Priorities for Student Competence in Ten Fields of Professional Study." Paper presented at the Association for the Study of Higher Education, San Antonio, Texas, February 20-23, 1986a.

Stark, J. S., Lowther, M. A., and Hagerty, B.M.K. "Faculty Roles and Role Preferences in Ten Fields of Professional Study." Paper presented at the American Educational Research Association, San Francisco, April 16-20, 1986b.

Stark, J. S., Lowther, M. A., and Hagerty, B.M.K. "Outcomes of Professional Preparation." *ERIC/ASHE Higher Education Reports.* Washington, D.C.: Association for the Study of Higher Education, 1986c.

102

Stark, J. S., Lowther, M. A., Hagerty, B.M.K., and Orczyk, C. "A Conceptual Framework for the Study of Preservice Professional Programs in Colleges and Universities." *Journal of Higher Education*, 1986, *57* (3), 231-258.

Joan S. Stark is professor of higher education at the Center for the Study of Higher and Postsecondary Education at the University of Michigan. Currently, she is also director of the Professional Preparation Project and of the National Center for Research to Improve Postsecondary Teaching and Learning (NCRIPTAL). Previously, she was dean of the School of Education at the University of Michigan.

The editor summarizes the ideas in this volume.

Concluding Notes and Further Readings

Mary Ann F. Rehnke

Woven through the preceding chapters are several themes that deserve special attention by the campus administrator contemplating the addition of a new curriculum. The advice of these authors is as follows:

1. Do what is best for *your* institution. With many campuses adding career programs, the pressure to do what everyone is doing may be great. However, review the strengths of your current curriculum, faculty, and mission as well as long-range plans for your institution to determine whether a specific career program is an appropriate addition to your college or university curriculum.

2. Avoid a narrow definition of career preparation. According to Heraclitus you cannot step into the same stream twice. Professions and the society in which they exist change too rapidly for students to receive during four years of college an education for their complete work life. A broad education preparing them to deal with the changes in their profession and society will serve them better.

3. Gather data about the need for the program widely. Go beyond the sources you would consult for creating a new liberal arts major. In addition to the sources suggested in the planning chapter, valuable data may also be obtained from the local chamber of commerce, the profession itself, or state planning commissions.

M.A.F. Rehnke (ed.). *Creating Career Programs in a Liberal Arts Context.*
New Directions for Higher Education, no. 57. San Francisco: Jossey-Bass, Spring 1987.

4. Avoid premature burial of a proposed program. It may appear that a curriculum is too expensive or that faculty for that field cannot be found. Do a short version of the feasibility study described in the planning chapter to evaluate numerous factors before deciding to abandon consideration of a program proposal.

5. Involve key faculty, administrators, and community representatives *early* in the development of the program. Their ideas will create a sound program, and their support will assist in the adoption and implementation of the new major.

6. Give attention during the program planning stage to assessment, faculty development, and creating compatibility with the liberal arts programs. These areas may seem to be ones that can be addressed later after the program is approved by all official bodies, but including these topics in the planning process will avoid potential problems. It is easier and more appropriate to include assessment in the program from the beginning. Faculty development concerns such as faculty needs for new advising skills or retraining to support career offerings if explored during program planning will strengthen the new major and perhaps gain faculty support rather than criticism. Also, the wise campus administrator will have created forums for the discussion of compatibility between the liberal arts and the new career program before their faculties can divide the campus into two warring camps.

7. Consult experts when creating the new curriculum. If the program is represented by an accreditation body, contact them through the office indicated on the chart in Chapter Six for advice in building a strong program. Create an advisory panel of professionals from your region in the proposed new field. They will have ideas about skills the new program should develop and will serve as a source of future support for the program when internships for students or guest speakers are needed.

8. Strengthen the support services for career programs on campus. The placement office, student cooperative, and career counseling services will have additional demands placed on them.

Additional references might prove helpful in the planning process. Those interested in the recent catalysts of the career movement would enjoy James Hitchcock's "The New Vocationalism" in *Change* (1973, 5 (3), 46-50). Three social theories are offered as an explanation of the increased interest in careers by Robert E. Roemer in "Vocationalism in Higher Education: Explanations from Social Theory," a paper presented at the 1980 annual meeting of the Association for the Study of Higher Education.

To gather data in the early stages of the planning process about other institutions that offer the proposed major, consult the *Index of Majors* published each year by the College Board. *The College Handbook*, another College Board publication, describes three thousand two- and four-year colleges and might prove helpful in determining which institutions comparable to yours offer the proposed major.

Ideas for strengthening the career education component of the college may be found in the Jossey-Bass *New Directions for Education, Work, and Careers* series edited by Lewis C. Solomon from 1978–1979; *Career Education in Colleges: A Guide for Planning Two- and Four-Year Occupational Programs* by Norman C. Harris and John F. Grede, (San Francisco: Jossey-Bass, 1977); *Designing Careers* by Norman C. Gysbers and Associates (San Francisco: Jossey-Bass, 1984); and the *Journal for Career Education*.

As the college develops the curriculum, "Program: A Focus on Purpose and Performance" by Arthur Levine in *Opportunity in Adversity* by Arthur Levine, Janice S. Green, and Associates (eds.) (San Francisco: Jossey-Bass, 1986) deals with myths about the curriculum and aids in finding the most appropriate program for the institution. Processes proven to be helpful for developing career programs at junior colleges are described by Jack Harris in "A Synopsis of Keeping Occupational Education Current: Formation and Evaluation—DACUM," a paper presented at the Great Lakes Regional Conference of the American Technical Education Association in November 1982 by Jack Harris, and "Curriculum Design and Evaluation: An Employer-Center Action Approach," a paper presented at the Annual Forum of the Association for Institutional Research in April 1980 by Mantha Vlahos Mehallis. Journals for the profession, such as the *Journal of Education for Social Work* or the *Journal of Engineering Education*, frequently contain articles about curriculum design for their disciplines. To identify competencies and attitudes common to many professional programs, Joan S. Stark, Malcolm A. Lowther, and Bonnie M. K. Hagerty have written *Responsive Professional Education: Balancing Outcomes and Opportunities* (ASHE-ERIC Higher Education Report, no. 3. (Washington, D.C.: Association for the Study of Higher Education, 1986).

For additional resources on assessment, consult *Assessment in American Higher Education: Issues and Contexts* edited by Clifford Adelman (Washington, D.C.: U.S. Government Printing Office, 1986) for the chapter on "Assessing Outcomes in Higher Education" by John Harris that includes addresses and telephone numbers of helpful contacts.

For ideas on integrating liberal learning and professional education, refer to "A Dialogue on Liberal Learning in Professional Education" (Washington, D.C.: Association of American Colleges, 1976), the proceedings of a dialogue held at Worcester Polytechnic Institute; *Liberal Learning and Career Preparation* by Mary Ann F. Rehnke, guest editor, in Current Issues in Higher Education (American Association for Higher Education, 1982–1983); and *Quality in Liberal Learning* by George W. Hazzard, in *The Forum for Liberal Education* 2 (Washington, D.C.: Association of American Colleges, 1979).

Most campuses have a search service that can be used in researching any of the topics covered in this sourcebook. If one is not available, the Educational Resources Information Center (Clearinghouse on Higher Education, Suite 630, One Dupont Circle, Washington, D.C. 20036, telephone 202-296-2597) could be utilized.

With these resources and the information provided in each of the chapters, campuses can create career programs in a liberal arts context that will prepare students for a useful role in society.

Mary Ann F. Rehnke is director of annual programs at the Council of Independent College.

Index

A

Abrams, A. L., 3, 39, 47
Accreditation, 49, 52; bodies for, 54-61; and certification and licensure, 51-53; costs of, 53, 62; institutional and specialized, 49-51
Accrediting Bureau of Health Education Schools, 56
Accrediting Council on Education in Journalism and Mass Communication, 55
Advising, academic, 36-37; strategies for, 85-86
Affordability, of new career program, 24-25. *See also* Finances
Age Discrimination Act, 43
Allen v. Lewis-Clark State College, 40, 47
American Assembly of Collegiate Schools of Business, 54
American Association of Bible Colleges, 50
American Association of University Professors, 40, 41, 47
American Board of Funeral Service Education, 51
American College Testing (ACT): Assessment and Interest Inventory, 72; Career Planning Program, 72; Discover, 72; tests for assessment, 68
American Council for Construction Education, 51, 54
American Council on Pharmaceutical Education, 60
American Dental Association, 58
American Dietetic Association, 55
American Home Economics Association, 51, 55
American Library Association, 56
American Medical Association, 52, 57
American Optometric Association, 59
American Physical Therapy Association, 60
American Society of Landscape Architects, 59

American Veterinary Medical Association, 51
Anderson, O., 78, 81
Anthony, W. P., 37
Assessment(s), 67; basic procedures for, 68-69; building, into credit system, 70; in career program, 66; to describe graduates' abilities, 67-68; developing effective, 70-71; mentor program as part of, 72-73; problems in testing for, 69-70; references on, 105; for student guidance, 71-72
Association of Advanced Rabbinical and Talmudic Schools, 56
Association of American Colleges, 96, 97, 101
Association of Independent Colleges and Schools, 50
Association of Theological Schools in the United States and Canada, 50
Astin, A., 76, 81
Axelson, L., 78, 81

B

Bagshaw, M., 42, 47
Baldwin, R. G., 3, 83, 87, 88, 90
Barr, 19
Bellak v. Franconia College, 40, 47
Birmingham-Southern College, 88
Board of Regents v. Roth, 40, 47
Boucher, W. I., 31, 37
Bradshaw v. Rawlings, 45, 47
Browzin v. Catholic University of America, 41, 47
Buchanan, 19
Bureau of Labor Statistics, 6, 35

C

California State College at San Bernadino, 13
California State University at Long Beach, 87
Career: choices of minority students, 76-77; choices of women, 77-78

107

preparation, 14; support services,
36-37, 80. *See also* Minorities;
Women
Systems approach, to instruction,
66-67, 73

T

Tennent, G., 16, 20
Terborg, J. R., 78, 81
Thibadoux, G. M., 53, 63
Traditional professional competences
(TPCs), 94-98
Trent, W., 76, 81
Tucker, M. S., 1, 2, 5, 11

U

U.S. Department of Education, 63;
accrediting bodies recognized by,
50-51
U.S. Department of Health and
Human Services, 36
U.S. Department of Labor, 35-36

V

Values, changes in, 7, 8
Veblen, T., 15
Virginia, University of, 17
Vocationalism: debate on, 14-15; dis-
senters to, 19; history of debate on,
15-16. *See also* Education, career

W

Western Association of Schools and
Colleges, 50
Winstead, P. C., 2, 29, 30, 37
Women: career choices of, 77-78; characteristics of successful, 78; institutional responses to, 77; recommendations for retaining, 78-80
Work force, future demand for educated, 5-6

Y

Yale, 16, 17